LEADING THE
Real Estate
Transaction

JOHN C. RITCHIE

Cover home built by: Michael Bates Homes
Member *Southern Living* Custom Builder Program

Cover Photo by: Studio 102

ISBN: 1-4196-9037-X
ISBN-13: 9781419690372

Visit www.booksurge.com to order additional copies.

To Contact the author: jcr@realestatelearning.com

Table of Contents

LEADING THE REAL ESTATE TRANSACTION

In every real estate transaction someone has to lead the process. Leadership may be shared if everyone understands how it works. However, in most cases, someone takes charge and becomes the driving force behind successfully completing the process and closing the transaction. Given the opportunity to lead, one should prefer to lead or share leadership than to follow or, worse, do nothing to aid in the process.

So how does one gain leadership? This book will explain and illustrate the processes necessary for gaining leadership and taking the lead in the transaction.

The leader of the process negotiates the box or comfort zone from which decisions can be made by all parties to the transaction. Once everyone is in the same box, the transaction time line begins. The objective of leadership is to keep everyone in the same box until closing by facing conflict as it occurs and resolving problems before they gain any momentum.

Leaders focus on finishing the transaction with all parties satisfied that they got what they agreed upon with minimum effort on the client's part. Leaders manage behind the scenes most of what happens and minimize client anxiety not by making decisions but by supplying appropriate solutions to choose from that are acceptable to all.

Managing a real estate transaction can sometimes seem like trying to herd cats. Leaders operate on the premise that the seller wants to sell and the buyer wants to buy. Everything in between is simply a matter of clarifying details and defining solutions in order to achieve the objective.

The first step of managing the process is to understand something about people and how they make decisions or negotiate. To understand others, people must first understand their own processes for making decisions or negotiating.

All decisions are made on a sliding bar that weighs the emotional and logical factors that influence the decision. Even if no one else is involved, people negotiate within themselves when weighing the consequences and benefits of a decision.

The bar shifts depending on the priority, and perceived importance of the decision slides the bar from emotion to logic. Once fact-finding or logic is satisfied, all decisions are made at the emotional level. What that means is that once we can defend our decision, we do what we want to do.

Illustration...

You want to buy a new flat screen TV. You have a budget in mind (logical). You go to the local electronics store to see what your budget will allow (logical). You find that you can purchase a 52" TV that looks great (emotional). You go home and research the information on the TV as well as other brands and pricing at other stores because the salesperson has told you that the store will meet any price on the TV (logical). You find a price $300 lower, go back to the store, and purchase the TV you wanted (emotional) convinced that instead of spending $1,600, you saved $300 (very emotional).

You could have either bought the TV you wanted with no research just because you liked it (a very emotional response) or you could have done more research, including asking friends, etc. (more logical), but in this case, you satisfied your responsible side and got what you wanted.

So how does this relate to real estate? **The process for buying real estate works exactly the same. People acquire enough logical information to justify an emotional decision.**

Think about some of your clients and how they made either a listing or buying decision. List the emotional and the logical steps in their processes.

_____

_____

_____

List the similarities regarding the decisions:

_____

_____

_____

List the differences in how they made decisions:

_____

_____

_____

How can this information help you more effectively work with sellers or buyers?

_____

_____

_____

People make decisions on a sliding scale of emotion and logic.

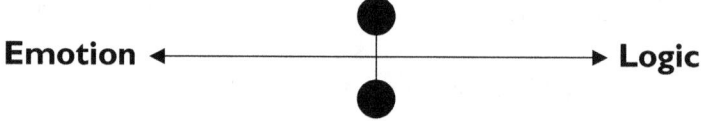

Emotion ◄—————————————► **Logic**

People negotiate in the same manner depending on how much they rely on emotion or logic to guide their decision making. Decision making determines how people negotiate; people negotiate by the same processes that drive their decision making. An agent has the responsibility of accurately assessing the client's decision-making process in order to guide the transaction in a manner that is comfortable to all parties. It is in the best interest of all parties, including the agent, to do so.

From the decision-making/negotiating perspective, people fall somewhere on the scale between highly emotional and highly logical. Negotiating and decision making tend to move on a sliding scale based on people's emotional and logical approaches. Some people make decisions based on what they want at the moment, others might decide to take action only when it is logical to do so. People place differing emphasis on the emotional or logical elements based on the importance of the decisions and the perceived and real impact of decisions.

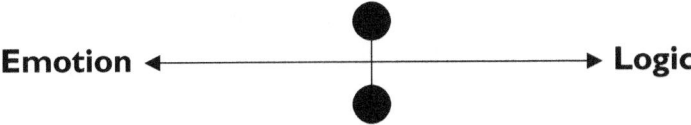

Emotion ◄———————————► **Logic**

Some think that either they or the sales process can drive or negotiate people to the emotional side of the slide bar. They understand that decisions are always made on at the emotional level once the logical needs have been satisfied. However, they falsely assume that logical need can be bypassed instead of understanding how to satisfy those needs. This method tires to disguise or bypass logical needs by increasing the emotional desire. This rarely works and most clients recognize this approach and view it as highly manipulative. They resent the disregard for what they have defined as logical need and lose trust in the person trying to use this tactic.

Only the most emotional people will make a decision without some fact-finding. Actually, it is their nature to make decisions in this manner, not salesmanship or someone else's opinion. Totally logical people, when pressured to make an emotional decision, will not do so until the facts are determined. When under emotional pressure they will not make a decision or enter the negotiating process. A professional agent asks questions and listens to determine just where the client's comfort level is in order to meet the client's needs.

This book will explore understanding how to meet the clients' logical needs in order to release them to do what they want to do. Professional agents should strive to understand what tools they have to work with and how to effectively apply these tools to best match the needs and decision-making styles of their clients. There is no "totally right" method since all people, including the agent, are different in how they approach decision making and negotiating.

Never count on a totally emotional decision from anyone and always be prepared to supply just enough logic for the decision or negotiating to occur.

UNDERSTANDING PEOPLE

People make decisions and negotiate; therefore, understanding how their emotional/logical makeup affects both is extremely important.

Highly emotional people tend to:

- Make quick decisions based on what is in front of them at the time
- Do not require much in the way of facts
- Invest highly in verbal presentations
- Put too much faith in relationships that have not earned trust
- Often suffer from "buyer's remorse"
- Can feel that they are victims of others when they are actually victims of self
- Become evasive when pressed for a decision
- Maintain control by evading decisions and changing the subject
- Do not manage boundaries well
- Do not define risk well
- Often display low assertiveness
- Will often base decisions on pleasing others
- Appearance or perception is more important than reality

Also...

- They are the fun people
- They are highly resilient
- They are energetic
- They like and are liked by people
- They are visionary regarding ideas

Highly emotional people have trouble managing time lines or processes. They tend to act quickly to resolve problems and to feel good. Unfortunately, the "feel good" does not last long and they often suffer from buyer's remorse. These people rely heavily on others to tell them how to make a decision and therefore often see themselves as victims of others instead of victims of their own behavior. They often attempt to make decisions that please others because they think this makes others like them even if others do not justify this level of consideration. This desire to be liked can make them vulnerable to those who would take advantage of the situation.

Under pressure, highly emotional people tend to become indecisive or seem evasive. They see talking as relationship building and valuable. When they feel pressed to make decisions, they feel that the other person is becoming harsh or pushy. If they are forced to make decisions prematurely, they will often back out later and avoid the experience with the same person again.

Highly emotional types are low in assertiveness. People with these tendencies tend to try to convince others with lots of words, often without fact or logical progression. They think of themselves as assertive when they can actually come across as disorganized, wordy, or without substance. When challenged regarding the facts behind the words, they can become defensive or simply avoid the confrontation totally. Their avoidance can sometimes result in a complete change of subject to avoid answering direct questions or addressing conflict. When helping these types with decision making or negotiating, it is important to stay focused. They can easily confuse others to the point that the whole process has to be redefined. If asked to participate, someone may have to interrupt them mid sentence to regain control. Time is of no importance to these types if they feel that everyone else is enjoying the conversation. In reality, their lack of direction or respect for time wears others out.

Also these are fun people who attract others. Their lack of concern about details or boundaries provides tremendous resilience when things do not work out. "If at first you don't succeed, try, try again" might be their rally point. They like the energy they associate with new ideas or direction outside of what they consider to be boring predictable processes. These people always have something going on in their lives that provides an interesting story to the other types. They are new-idea people and often visionary in their approach to life. These people are often founders or inventors and can be highly effective if they surround themselves with others who provide direction for their energy and ideas. Highly emotional types are classic sales-profile people although their attention to details and time usually needs managing.

Illustration...

Agent Joan is conducting a listing presentation to Bill and Susan. Bill is very friendly and offers even more information about the house than Joan is expecting. The presentation is going so well that Joan is sure that she will obtain the listing. As Joan is completing the presentation, she asks Bill and Susan if they have any questions regarding the presentation. They both say no. Joan begins to explain the contract and notices that Bill is becoming a little uncomfortable. Joan presents the competitive market analysis and asks Bill and Susan what they would like to list the house for. Bill asks Joan what she thinks. Joan replies, "I can supply the information, however, the list price is up to you." Bill then says, "I understand that the commission rate is 6%." Joan says, "No, Bill, there is no set rate, as that would violate the law. However, that said, I will be willing to list the property for 6% if that is agreeable." Joan then says that she would like to list the property for six months based on the inventory available and rate of sale for properties similar to Bill and Susan's.

Bill then says, "That seems fair to me. Let Susan and me think about it and get back to you."

Joan leavers the presentation and calls Bill back the next day. Bill says, "I was in the grocery store last night after the presentation and ran into my old buddy whose daughter is getting a real estate license and will be ready to list in two weeks. She is living at home and cannot move out until she makes some money. I want to help out, so I am going to list with her. I want you to know that you made a great presentation."

Exercise...
What could Joan do now?

_____

_____

_____

What could she have done at the presentation?

_____

_____

_____

Joan could have pushed a little harder to sign the listing at the presentation. She might have said, "While I am here, let's finish the paperwork. I will call tomorrow and if you decide not to proceed, we can void the listing. This might have been enough to keep Bill from considering his friend's daughter. However, by using this approach, Joan would still have taken a chance of pushing too hard and still may have lost the listing. Bill's decision is based on "sharing his wealth" with his friend instead of protecting his investment. Although his approach is noble, it may not be in his best interest. For Bill, helping his friend's daughter represents a higher purpose. He will probably regret his decision later, but for now he will feel good about what he has done. He makes the decision because he perceives it as the right thing to do and because he wants his friend to "like" him.

Types with some balance of emotion and logic tend to overbalance to either the emotional or logical side, which presents certain decision-making and negotiating tendencies:

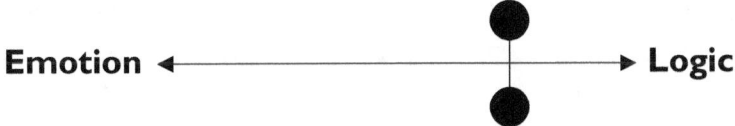

Emotion ◄————————————————► **Logic**

Overbalanced logical types tend to:

-   Make calculated decisions based on what serves them best
-   Use time to their advantage
-   Use the logic or emotion of others to their benefit
-   Size people up quickly in regard to strengths and weaknesses
-   Use verbal and fact to their advantage
-   Work to win/lose decisions (negotiating results in giving more than getting)
-   Maintain control by their dominant personalities
-   Will steamroll if allowed
-   See managing risk as an advantage to them
-   Be highly assertive
-   Make decisions based on what serves them

Also...

-   They are the "go to" people
-   They are highly productive
-   They are results focused
-   They are valued by peers
-   They are visionary at how to produce results

People overbalanced to the logical side will take care of themselves first. When faced with decisions, these types tend to research enough to satisfy their logical side before seeking verbal input. They will use written material, friends, Internet, or any reliable resource before accepting a sales presentation or after the presentation to check it out. These types use the research to gain an advantage in decision making. They will quiz a presenter to see if he or she knows a product. These types know that if the presenter cannot defend a product or service based on fact that the value is diminished and there is an opening to negotiate. These types are good poker players; they do not expose a position unless it gains some advantage for them. They will seldom expose the fact that they want a product. Making the best possible deal is as important as obtaining a product. Often these people will appear to take charge and intimidate others to get their way. They will walk away from a deal that is not to their advantage. These people are highly aware of their options in decision making and use their options effectively. These types know how to appear to be likable as part of their nature. They prefer for other parties to the decision to like them and will use the emotion of others to gain advantage.

People of this nature can appear to be highly assertive. They usually have either the facts to back up their position or the confidence to seem to have the facts. Their self-confidence, command of logic/facts, and verbal skills afford the assertive position. They are focused on how to meet their needs or goals even at the expense of others.

Also these types are the go to people in an organization. They are highly skilled in evaluating people and situations and quick to understand how to use processes that channel energy into results. They are highly valued by their peers for their ability to make good decisions quickly under fire. This type is good at channeling energy. Success is important to overbalanced logicals and they are uncomfortable when they do not perceive themselves to be winning. They are good managers of time, people, and processes. Logical people use words to maintain control of both the emotional and logical elements of decision making and negotiating. They do not waste time and stay focused on what they perceive to be important in meeting their logical and emotional needs.

Illustration...

Agent Bill shows Mark and Jean houses on their visit to his market. As they are finishing up, Mark and Jean tell Bill that they have found three properties that will work for them. They lay out this strategy for purchasing a home.

They tell Bill that they will write three offers in order of preference. They instruct Bill to present the offers, one at a time, to each seller as a final offer. They also instruct Bill to tell each agent as the offer is presented about their situation and that if offer "A" is not accepted, that Bill is instructed to withdraw the offer and move to offer "B" or "C." They also tell Bill that when they get off the plane in six hours, they expect for him to have a contract on one of the three properties.

Exercise...

How should Bill proceed?

_____

_____

_____

Is this a workable strategy? Why or why not?

_____

_____

_____

Based on Mark and Jean's directions, Bill should say exactly what they have told him and instruct listing agents to relay the same information to their sellers. Bill has the opportunity to train each seller's agent regarding the presentation of the offer. Each seller's agent should appreciate the facts because the agent can present the offer in a way that does not position the agent as the "bad guy." The offer can then be presented without emotion, requiring only a yes or no answer from sellers. With the facts, each seller's agent can keep clients from worrying about what to counter and focus strictly on whether or not to accept the offer as presented.

The main issue for the seller's agent in this illustration is to stick to the facts and stay focused on the yes or no aspect of the offer. If the seller's agent allows the seller to get emotional about the offer, the decision will be more difficult to make.

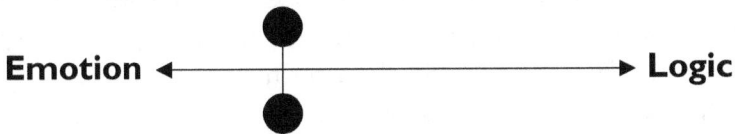

Overbalanced emotional types tend to:

- Base decisions on what is best for everyone
- Value both emotion and logic
- Value both verbal and fact-based material
- Back out later if pushed into a decision
- Listen more than participate
- Not need to be in control
- Appear to allow others to dominate their decision making

- Minimize risk by studying and listening
- Prefer more of a caretaker position than assertiveness
- Prefer decisions that please everyone
- Not need a front-and-center position

Also...

- They are the behind-the-scene producers
- They are great at finishing production projects
- They are good at following instructions
- They are good evaluators
- They are sometimes overlooked by peers
- They are visionary at finishing details

Those overbalanced to the emotional side tend to see a bigger picture in decision making than the other types. These types tend to be caretakers in their approaches and are willing to sacrifice a win/lose position to a win/win to keep everyone at peace with the deal. These people rely on both fact and logic in decision making and are more introspective in weighing how to proceed. They tend to minimize the risk factors in decision making by taking their time to digest what they hear and learning before making decisions. Immediacy is not as important as minimizing risk. They tend to begin fact-finding before allowing themselves to become so emotionally attached that they do not maintain their logical integrity. If it means losing an opportunity by taking too long in the decision-making process, they can accept that outcome. "Like" is important to these types but only to the extent that it serves to provide an equitable decision. They will research the facts and factor in people and emotion only when the people and emotion support the facts they believe to be true. They respect others as long as others demonstrate integrity in the process.

Their cautious nature in decision making can be misinterpreted by other types as indecisive, nonassertive, or unable to make a decision. However, once these types are allowed to take their time to research and ask the questions they need answered, patience pays off in that they are extremely loyal to those who serve their nature.

Also these types are great at follow-up or as project managers and will see a project through to finish. Sometimes their quiet nature causes this type to be overlooked by peers because they do not crave the spotlight. However, these types are highly valuable and need to be recognized for their efforts. They know what is going on in the process but sometimes need to be asked before they will contribute what they know. They are good listeners and evaluators and, if asked, have much to contribute regarding how to do things better.

Illustration...

Susan is showing homes to Mary and Ed. As she progresses through the day and begins to ask which of the properties they like best, neither seems to have found the right house although several seem to exactly meet the needs that Susan determined during her fact-finding interview. After showing all of the properties, Susan asks for feedback on the properties. Mary and Ed say they liked some of the properties but have not found the right one yet. Susan says, "Help me out. Based on what we saw today, what needs to change?"

Mary says, "I am not sure, we just need to see some more houses tomorrow to help us decide." Susan asks, "Do you want to change the criteria of our search or the price range?" Mary says, "No. We just need to see more of the same."

Exercise...
What should Susan do?

_____

_____

_____

There are two issues here. What Susan should do and what she should not do. Susan should decide if she can continue to work with Mary and Bill. If the answer is yes, Susan needs to be very careful about her attitude and tone of voice. If Susan continues, and she should because Mary and Ed are going to buy a house, she needs to be patient and understand that she cannot force a decision. There could be a tendency during the next day's showings to begin to pressure Mary and Bill into better qualifying their decision. Mary and Ed are probably going to look at quite a few homes and when they see the right one, even if they cannot clearly communicate just what that is, they will buy. Susan is going to have to give up control of the process until she better understands what Mary and Ed want. For now, they want to look at more properties. It is a time for Susan to listen carefully before asking questions and allow Mary and Ed to establish their comfort with the decision. If Susan tries to control the decision or time line at this point, she may lose her clients if they feel pressured.

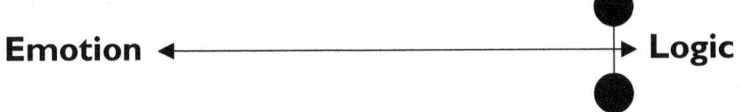

Highly logical types tend to:

- Sometimes seem cold and hard to "figure out"
- Depend on facts
- Not be pushed into a decision
- See relationships as a liability in decision making
- Prefer written documents as opposed to verbal presentation
- Not be rushed into a decision outside their comfort zone
- Maintain control of the process by knowledge
- Try to remove risk by reliance on facts only
- Base assertiveness on a right or proven position
- Base decisions on fact; fact-based decisions should be best for everyone

Also...
- They are the knowledge people
- They are the resources for facts and figures
- They are respected by peers
- they are visionary in making activities worthwhile (profitable)

Highly logical persons can appear to be the hardest to figure out. These types listen but demand backup to verbal. They like facts and written documentation regarding promises, features or any other facts affecting their decision making. They take notes either mentally or in writing to document anything said that affects a decision. These people indicate that they do not need or want to build a relationship in order to make a decision. In fact, these types are turned off by flashy presentations that they feel are not backed up by fact. If they think that a presentation is without substance, they will lose trust quickly and pursue another avenue for decision making. Highly logicals prefer respect as opposed to "like." They believe that respect can be earned based of fact and personal integrity. Highly logical people prefer to make a decision without worrying about who likes whom. They place little value on anything that diverts attention from the facts affecting a decision.

Highly logical people can be perceived as extremely assertive, especially to those who need little logical support in decision making. They can seem tedious in their desire to research all of the facts before a decision is made. Until these people are satisfied that a decision is proven to be right, they will not be persuaded. Once they are sure about a decision or position, they will seldom change their minds. Even if facts to the contrary are presented, the case will have to be overwhelming to convince them to change course after a decision is made.

Also these types are considered to be the fact or resource people in the organization. They are respected and sometimes even considered intimidating by their peers. They move through the fluff to the meat quickly and are focused on the bottom line. These types evaluate from a position of "if we do it, what will it be worth?" Sometimes they are purposely excluded from the decision-making process if emotion is the primary factor in a decision. Highly logicals offset the emotion of the moment with their logical questions. Although sometimes seen as the deal breakers, they are actually the field levelers by injecting the purest form of logic into the decision.

Illustration...

John is interviewing Linda by phone about the visit she and husband Richard will be making to purchase a home. Linda seems very cordial and says she has everything written down regarding their needs in a new home. After the interview, as John begins to research properties, it is apparent to him that some compromise will have to be made to accommodate Linda and Richard's needs. Assuming that Linda and Richard are both high logicals, what should John do? He has two days before Linda and Richard arrive to begin their search.

Exercise...

What should John do?

_____

_____

_____

Is there any risk in his decision?

_____

_____

_____

What does John stand to gain?

_____

_____

_____

If indeed John has determined Linda and Richard to be high logicals, he needs to call them back and discuss the possible compromises with them in advance. (He needs to take this step no matter which type of person he thinks they are.) By making the call, John will gain trust as well as more efficiently use the time for looking.

If John does not make the call, he will probably not show Linda and Richard properties they will consider, waste time, and lose credibility.

The risk is that Linda and Richard will not believe that John can meet their exact needs. However, there is a stronger possibility that they will respect John's call and trust will increase. Always remember that when buyers have not visited a new market, they will base housing needs on what is familiar to them from where they live. Most buyers are prepared to compromise on some of their needs when making a move to a new location.

Exercise...

Think about each of these types.

Which tendencies best describe you?

_____

_____

_____

Which are least like you?

_____

_____

_____

Which are the hardest for you to work with?

_____

_____

_____

How can you improve working with all types of people?

_____

_____

_____

The different tendencies of people are all valuable. In fact, most people exhibit tendencies from all types depending on the circumstances and how much emotion or logic is deemed necessary in making a decision. It is important for an agent to have a good understanding of "self" and how to relate to and communicate with those who do or do not evaluate a situation the same way. It is not important to mirror the tendencies of others; however, it is important to value how they think and contribute to the decision-making or negotiating process.

Once it is acknowledged that people are different, it is easy to understand why they make decisions differently as well as negotiate differently. Different types of people will also respond differently to various negotiating tactics.

> _Without trust, meaningful communication does not exist._

It is most important to understand how people will act in order to gain trust and therefore communicate in a manner that is comfortable to them. Without understanding people, real estate agents will not be able to gain leadership of the process because their clients and colleagues will not trust them. Without trust, meaningful communication does not exist.

So how does this work...

The above tendencies will determine not only how decisions are made but also determine the comfort area for decision making.

How Decision Making Occurs

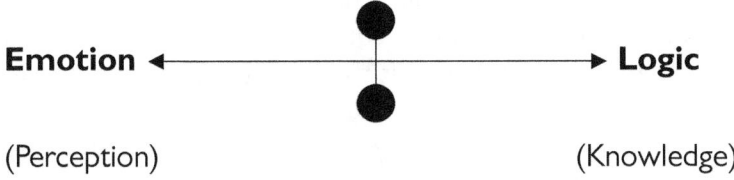

Emotion ◄─────────────────► **Logic**

(Perception)   (Knowledge)

Knowledge and Perception

Knowledge is the fact base that is used to make a decision and represents the logical side of the slide bar. Perception is the emotional side of the bar representing what someone wants to believe to be true in order to support a decision. Balancing the two represents the injection of wisdom.

Knowledge is the logical fact base. Perception is the emotional side that allows us to do what we want to do. Applying wisdom balances the two.

Once the decision-making process begins, all people obtain some factual information from some resource. Once the logical is satisfied, people always make the decision at an emotional level. In other words, people gather enough information to justify doing what they want to do. Wisdom or lack thereof defines the process and ultimately the results.

Illustration...

I answered my telephone one evening about a week before Thanksgiving. The gentleman who was calling introduced himself as a bank employee associated with my home equity credit line. He said, "Good evening, we at the bank notice that you have a substantial available balance in your home equity account. Is there anything you would like to have?"

What a question to ask as I watched my perfectly good projection TV. I immediately had a vision of a new flat screen TV on the wall.

Exercise...

Think about each of the tendencies of people that have been discussed.

- What type of person did the bank employee hope he had contacted?

_____

_____

_____

- What responses was he expecting?

_____

_____

_____

Think about each of the people types. Each would probably respond differently.

A **highly emotional type** would be the best recipient for this type of call. The bank will supply the resources, he has some desire, and he can make a decision that will provide immediate gratification. He probably will agree to get what he wants over the phone but might not follow through once he thinks about the decision later. The real decision will probably be based on the next person he talks to. If it is his friend who would like to watch the Thanksgiving ball games on a new TV, he will probably gain enough support to buy the TV. If it is possibly someone who says, "Why would you spend $2,000 on a new TV when the one we have is fine?" He may not move forward. It is likely that he will think about both responses and try to figure out how to please his friend and justify the purchase to the other party. Possibly he will buy the TV and have it installed hoping that the one who disagreed will be so happy to see the TV that the objection will be forgotten.

An **overbalanced logical type** would view this opportunity differently. This type would know that the resources were available in his account prior to the call. He would think about the TV and try to decide if there was any advantage to buying it. His thought pattern would probably cause him to do some research into TVs concerning potential values and what would be available. He would probably do his research and determine what he would buy and wait until the Thanksgiving sales to see if he could obtain a deal on the TV. This type would gain as much pleasure about getting a great deal on a TV as the actual purchase.

A **highly logical type** might simply say to the bank, "Thank you very much for the offer, but do you think I am crazy?" This type knows to the penny what is in his account. Why would anyone in his right mind buy a TV when he has one? He would probably wonder how the bank could justify paying someone to make these calls. The idea of buying something just because you could borrow the money makes no logical sense to this type.

An **overbalanced emotional type** would probably think about the opportunity. He would also be aware of the fact that he could borrow the money. However, this type would possibly do some research, talk to other people, and weigh the decision. He would think, "Do I want a TV? Do I need a TV? What are the benefits and the consequences to this decision? It would be a toss-up regarding his final decision. After weighing all the facts, he will make the decision that makes the most sense based on his desire and need as he sees them.

So at least three of the types would consider the decision and move forward based on how best to satisfy their emotional and logical needs. The point is that not only will each type make the decision differently; individuals might come to different conclusions in the end.

Each type of person will rely on his or her personal traits to determine how a decision will be made, first relying to some extent on knowledge—knowledge being defined as some method of finding enough facts to satisfy logical needs. Sources of knowledge could include:

- Internet research
- Visit to the service or product vendor
- Brochures
- References from friends
- Expert advice

The list can include any resource that is considered valuable to the decision maker. The highly emotional type might use only verbal resources, whereas the highly logical might rely only on written material or someone he or she considers an expert. The problem is that even the most logical person has a logic bias to the resources he or she chooses. Once the person obtains all the information, his or her emotional side will still determine how to rate or value the information. Inevitably people choose to believe what works for them. That is where **perception** enters the decision-making process.

Perception is what we believe to be true and factual. If even the most logical decision maker at some point relies on his perception or interpretation of fact, then the most emotional decision maker will rely almost entirely on what he or she believes to be true with little effort dedicated to fact-finding.

For a real estate agent, this means working on truly understanding not only the tendencies of the people one is working with but also how they value the different aspects of the buying or selling process. Even if clients understand the process, their behaviors are not necessarily predictable.

Illustration...

In a buyer's market, Jeff meets with the Smiths to discuss listing their home. Jeff tells the Smiths that the market favors buyers and that it could easily take six months to find a buyer. The Smiths say they understand but are not comfortable with listing any longer than three months.

What should Jeff do?

_____

_____

_____

There is no right answer to this question. Jeff has shared the facts and the Smiths are unwilling to accept them.

Jeff can:

-   List the house and take the risk of it not selling
-   Thank the Smiths and decline the listing
-   Propose to list the home if the Smiths will agree to extend the listing if the house has not sold as long as Jeff is performing as promised.

However, as the three months pass and the house has not sold, the Smiths become anxious about the property and feel out of control. They are unwilling to reduce the price; what do you think they decide to do?

_____

_____

_____

That is right, change agents. Unfortunately the Smiths exercise the only option they feel they are willing to take. Jeff has done everything he said but still loses the listing. Facts would indicate continuing with Jeff but perception (emotional side) says that changing the agent will magically cause the house to sell.

Think about a recent decision you made.

How much was based on fact, how much or perception?

_____

_____

_____

Were you satisfied with the results of your decision?

_____

_____

_____

In retrospect, how would you approach the decision differently if you could do it over?

_____

_____

_____

When considering knowledge vs. perception in decision making, the importance of the decision will also have an impact on how each is valued. In most cases, the more important the decision, the more logical people become. The perception is that when more logic is applied, the emotional aspect is slowed down a bit.

If you were in a market deciding on which bottle of water you were going to buy, you might take a little time to make the decision. If you were in the desert without water for two days, you would drink any water you could find.

The real estate decision will vary almost as drastically depending on the attitude and values (emotion and logic) of the buyer toward the decision.

Illustration...

First-time buyers find a home they like. The home has two bedrooms and one bath. It is in fair condition although the fireplace does not work. The house is listed for $99,000 although the competitive analysis of the area shows the home worth approximately $90,000. Upon review of the buyers' application, a mortgage broker says they can secure a 100% loan for the property. The buyers like the idea since they have little cash and are living with parents.

Exercise...

What should the buyers' agent do or advise?

_____

_____

_____

What should the buyers do?

_____

_____

_____

Unfortunately the mortgage broker seems to be implying that since the buyers can have the house and meet their needs that they should act. The perception is that because they can have what they want, it is a good decision. The fact is that if the buyers purchase this property they will be have a deficit of $10K on the house, not even taking into account the repair of the fireplace, which could be as much as $5,000. Since the house has two bedrooms and one bath, it is a challenging property to sell as well.

The decision will be made by deferring to either the emotional "we can have a house" or the logical "this will be a risky financial decision" likely to have severe consequences in the long run.

You make the call as the buyers' agent. What would you do?

_____

_____

_____

Risk

The level of risk one is willing to take depends on the type of person making a decision. Risk is defined by the positive benefits or the negative consequences of our decisions. Risk will be influenced by how a person measures the fact or perception of fact regarding the benefits or consequences. Negotiators identify, minimize or maximize, eliminate or amplify either the benefits, consequences, or both in order to effectively manage the risk factor. Negotiating benefits everyone when all dimensions are considered fairly and the facts and perceptions are not manipulated to benefit one party at the expense of the others.

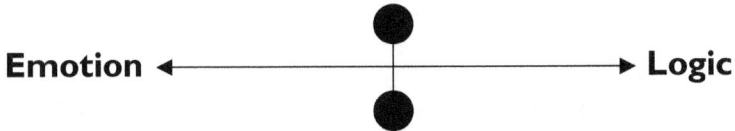

Emotion ◄———————┼———————► **Logic**

On the slide bar most people would prefer to remove risk from the decision-making process. We would like to be sure that we are making exactly the right decision every time. Unfortunately that is not possible.

Several factors influence risk, and these factors are valued by the tendencies of the person making the decision.

Risk Factors

Unscrupulous people will try to remove risk by:

- Questionable financing
- Embellishing the facts
- Outright fraud
- Intentionally misrepresenting the facts
- Omission of pertinent known facts
- Avoiding knowledge of pertinent facts

Defining the perceived and logical risk drives the decision-making process.

Beware if there is even a hint that any of these tactics are used to reduce risk. Reputable agents will avoid these tactics and instead assist in evaluating the following areas affecting and defining the risk factors. Shortcuts or questionable tactics are never good substitutes for ethical practices, reliable knowledge, and hard work.

Availability

Availability of the service or product we want impacts what we have to do to obtain what we want. In real estate, typically there will be either more properties available than prospective buyers or more prospective buyers than properties available.

If there are more properties than buyers:

- there is more to choose from and buyers can afford to be more selective

- Pricing will be lower, especially for buyers ready to close without other property to sell
- There may be extra incentives for the buyer
- Different options such as auctions or foreclosures are available
- Special financing may be available

A buyer in this market needs to do homework or retain an agent willing to do it. A little fact-finding goes a long way in this market and can save thousands of dollars.

A seller in this market needs to do everything possible to ensure that his or her property shows well. A seller should pre-inspect, make repairs, and clean up. Make the home as presentable as possible. All sellers should retain an agent who will give a brutal reality check of what it will take to sell the property, and then follow the instructions.

If there are more buyers than properties:

- Selection will be more limited. Buyers should define what they are willing to compromise in advance so they can make quick decisions.
- Prices may be higher, although qualified buyers with nothing to sell always have an advantage
- Options may be limited and require quick decisions in order to secure a property.

A buyer in this market needs to be prepared to compromise and act quickly.

The better the property shows in a seller's market, the more money it will bring. Sellers can afford to qualify the terms of an offer as well as the price in this type of market.

Resources

Resources are what it takes to cause the transaction to complete to closing.

Resources could include:

- Financial means   - Contractors
- Mortgage companies - Moving companies
- Title companies   - Utility providers
- Repair people
- Inspectors

Exercise...

What other resources could be added?

_____

_____

_____

Agents should accumulate a list of reliable resources to use in assisting buyers or sellers.

One of the most profound changes in acquiring real estate is the attitude of buyers toward ownership. Not that many years ago real estate financing required down payments in the range of 20%.

That accomplished:

1. A sense of ownership
2. Accumulation of equity

3.   Pride in ownership
4.   Reinvestment in the property in the form of repairs and updates

Ownership was something that people expected to accomplish in their lifetime instead of just accumulating more and more debt. Until recently ownership has been foundational to society. People who have accumulated some sense of ownership have always behaved differently than those who have nothing to lose. It will be interesting to see how this changes society over the next few years.

Today's real estate concept seems to be more one of usage almost to the extent that a home is to be used for a period of time and then replaced as the desire or need arises.

The idea of ownership seems to have gone away and financing more closely resembles a lease than a mortgage. We are now in an era of

1.   Lost sense of ownership
2.   Little if any accumulation of equity
3.   Use instead of ownership
4.   Little or no reinvestment

As long as appreciation covers all of the cost of replacement and income increases enough to pay the mortgage, this plan seems to work. If, however, either income or appreciation does not increase quickly enough, this plan falls apart.

Illustration...

A client is looking at a new home and comments to the agent, "This is the typical relocation home that we have bought on several moves. The walls are beige and the colors neutral. The feature package is what should be in a home of this price. The last home like this that we bought, we never hung any pictures because we knew we would be gone within twenty-four months."

This is a typical attitude in today's market. Buyers want relatively new homes that require little or no maintenance during their "user" period. They also now tend to borrow as much as possible with the intent of acquiring only the equity that comes from appreciation of the property. This approach will work for someone who has a plan and the cash to sell if necessary, regardless of the appreciation the market produces.

The problem is that many owners have purchased properties with no equity, no liquid savings, and no real possibility of dramatically increasing income, and **adjustable rate loans** that will escalate beyond what they can afford. If the market affords little or no appreciation, these people face a serious problem when attempting to sell in the future.

The fact that the seller has no cash and the buyer wants and needs to purchase a home with little or nothing invested is a bad combination. If the home needs repairs, neither the seller nor the buyer may have the disposable cash to complete the transaction. If no investment has been made to the property during the use by the seller, there may be no means to complete the repairs necessary for a sale to occur. Combine this with the fact that many sellers have used home equity loans in excess of the market value of their property to purchase disposable goods and an entirely different set of problems occurs.

As a result, there will be a reassessment of resources, and financial institutions will be forced to adjust how they lend in order to protect their investments. Some will suffer the consequences for over borrowing during the adjustment or will have to keep their current property until the climate of the market changes.

The solution will be that, once again, those who have available resources will be able to profit from the errors of others. There are significant opportunities available for those with cash. Even if sellers decide to sell for less than the market value, as long as they have equity after the sale, they should be able to recoup any apparent loss when they purchase.

Real estate agents will have to carefully evaluate the resources when listing or working with buyers in order to avoid this resource pitfall. Agents need to ask questions regarding the financial picture of the buyer or seller.

Buyer Question…

- Have you discussed your budget with a mortgage company?
o If the buyer indicates that he or she will need 100% financing or closing costs paid by the seller, there is a good chance that the buyer has little or no cash for the transaction.

Seller Questions…

- Is there a mortgage, second mortgage, or home equity loan on the property?
- What type loans are in place?
- How much equity do you think will be available after the loans are paid off?

- After costs and commission, will you have enough equity to meet your needs?
- Is there any room to negotiate from the list price?

Illustration...

A client has listed his home and an offer is made to purchase the property. The agent has asked the client what the mortgage balance is on the home. The client calls his mortgage company and determines that his balance will allow accepting the offer and paying the agent. Just before closing, the title company representative calls the agent and informs her that the company has discovered a home equity loan that was not considered. The net result is that the seller owes an additional $15,000 and will have to bring a $20,000 check to for the closing to occur.

Questions...

What are the seller's options?

_____

_____

_____

What are the buyer's options?

_____

_____

_____

If the buyer chooses to exercise his rights, the seller must deliver the property and possibly be liable for associated costs. However, that might not be feasible and might require the buyer to bring a lawsuit in order to procure the home. The seller may be forced to back out of the contract that he has to purchase another home as well, which creates another set of problems.

The buyer in this illustration needed a home quickly and therefore purchased another home.

The moral to this story is that agents must sometimes help prospective sellers understand the financial picture before investing time or effort in marketing a product that may not be salable. It is always better to have a complete understanding up front. Agents need a different set of questions to help the sellers understand their financial situations.

Agents need not think that the financial situations of sellers or buyers spell gloom and doom for real estate. Professional agents understand that the market, as well as buyer and seller profiles, are constantly changing. There are always opportunities for agents who are willing to understand the dynamics of the market and make the appropriate changes in their approaches to successfully address market changes.

> *No matter what the type of person, most want to hire a real estate professional, not become one.*

No matter what the type of person, most want to hire a real estate professional, not become one. Knowing the market and what it is going to take for a seller to sell or a buyer to buy is what clients want and need in an agent.

Most people expect the agent to take responsibility for hiring or managing the resources even though that expectation is misguided and can lead to significant problems if the agent does not explain how this process works. How much or how little the client chooses to be involved varies.

In most cases the real estate agent needs to prepare a list of what must be done and a time line to do it. The agent also needs to determine how much involvement the client wants to assume and the agent's role in the process. Many clients prefer to e-mail instructions and receive e-mail about results from agents. Check the time of day e-mails are sent. It seems that most of the time clients either start or end their days by sending out e-mails with instructions to agents. It becomes a great time management tool to be able to work on issues and respond on a timely basis instead of playing phone tag all day.

Added Value

Added value occurs when an agent clearly understands and performs as expected. Clients have usually had both good and bad experiences with Real Estate Agents. The easiest way to outperform expectations is to ask the client about both the good and bad experiences they have had. Once an agent knows what is considered to be good and bad behavior, it is easy to commit to a plan that pleases the client. The agent must then do what she is committed to do or trust will evaporate.

Product Added Value

How does an agent help a client determine product value?

Added value is why clients hire and pay agents.
If there was no added value; there would be no need for agents.

1.A competitive market analysis will provide the beginning facts to determine a base price of a property. Sometimes agents use this information solely to determine a price-by-the-pound target for listing a property. This is the most logical or analytical approach and adds no value for other factors that will influence a buyer's decision. This is an important step but does not present the entire picture of the property.

2.An appraisal also adds to the logical or analytical support for the listing price of a property. This information is also based on statistics using surrounding properties to establish a price based for the most part on square footage. Approaches 1 and 2 should produce very similar estimates.

3.Condition of the property and geographic area will either add or subtract from the analytical pricing of the home. How does the property show in relation to other like properties in the general geographic area? An agent must be familiar or become familiar with the area and how properties in the area appear from the curb.

Check list…

a. Are all of the properties in great condition?
b. Are the yards mowed?
c. Do they appear to be well cared for?
d. How many properties are distressed?
e. Are there any negative aspects to the appearance off other properties?

4.Condition of the interior of the home will have a huge impact on buyers.

a. Is the property clean?
b. Does it smell clean?

   c. Are there visual upgrades?

   d. Has the seller listed upgrades?

   e. Has the seller overspent on the upgrades for the neighborhood?

   f. Does everything work?

   g. Are there special features in the home?

5. Other factors of influence

   a. Schools

   b. Parks

   c. Special-needs facilities

   d. Shopping

   e. Special-interest services or products nearby

6. Comments from sellers

   a. Why do they like the home?

   b. Why do they like the neighborhood or area?

   c. What would they like to tell a prospective buyer?

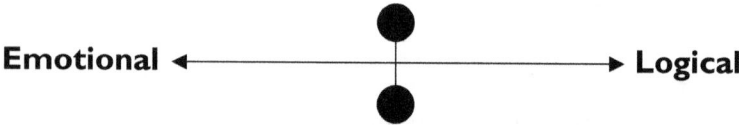

Emotional ←————————————→ **Logical**

All or some of these issues will have an effect on decision making. Some are emotional in nature and some are logical. Clients' tendencies will not only determine what is important but also how each of the issues will factor into their final decisions.

If a couple has no children, can an agent assume that schools will be unimportant in decisions? An agent can understand how any issue is valued only by asking the client about it. It is not important for an agent to go over every issue listed. What is important is for the agent to find out what is important to the client and research the information in advance so that answers are available and the agent knows where the facts can be found.

Illustration...

Agent Jones shows his clients the Browns properties that meet their needs. After the clients have successfully negotiated an offer to contract, Agent Jones asks, "What were the deciding factors in finalizing your decision?" The Browns say that they picked up a flyer in the property of choice with bullets about what the sellers liked about the property and why they hated to leave. Agent Jones asks what was important about the flyer. The Browns say there is a comment about how the neighborhood has weekly cookouts at the pool and everyone has a great time together. Agent Jones asks why that is so important. The Browns say they are anxious about the effect of the move on their children and that the cookouts will provide immediate opportunities to meet other children in the neighborhood.

Although several other homes would have met their needs well, the flyer heavily influenced the Browns' decision.

Exercise...

Do you think Agent Jones would consider including a flyer of this type in future listings?

_____

_____

_____

This is just one example of how creative agents can present their listings better than competitors. Although emotional in nature, a flyer of this type very well might clinch the decision. How could it hinder a decision?

How would you go about obtaining the information for a flyer of this type?

_____

_____

_____

Explain the benefits to the sellers and ask them to provide the information. The agent can then prioritize and format the points for prospective buyers.

Ask yourself, as an agent, are you familiar with each point on the check list?

_____

_____

_____

What others might you add to the list?

_____

_____

_____

Why is the information helpful when working with a prospective listing or buying client?

_____

_____

_____

The most important point here is to be different from the pack. Be ready to add value to the transaction that others overlook. Almost everyone knows a real estate agent in the market. In order to succeed, agents must provide added value to the decision-making process if they are to outperform their competitors.

Agent Added Value

What does an excellent real estate agent do for clients? A recent poll by the National Association of Realtors shows that the number one need of clients is for the agent to "manage" the real estate process. Clients do not want to become great real estate agents, they want to hire one.

Most clients are ignorant about how the real estate process works. They do not understand the layers of work, the knowledge required to interpret the factors influencing the transaction, the mental energy, or the financial investment agents provide on their behalf. Clients' experiences with real estate agents have varied from excellent to poor and most do not understand how to establish any sort of criteria for measuring and choosing an agent. Therefore, many choose an agent at random; the level of service is unpredictable, ranging from excellent to poor, as might be expected. Clients want to hire an agent whom they can trust. The way an agent earns trust is by demonstrating how he or she responds to clients' perceptions and facts and by competently managing the real estate process.

So how do excellent agents demonstrate their abilities to a prospective client? Most excellent agents know that much of what they do is actually transparent to the client. They want the client to experience an uneventful transaction from offer to closing so they manage the details **with permission** on behalf of their client. Knowledge is powerful but the ability to manage knowledge for a client is invaluable.

With as many real estate agents as there are in any market, buyers and sellers are actually deciding more as to whom they would like to share their wealth with through commissions. Agents should provide the best possible service to the clients in order for both to profit in a mutually acceptable manner. Agents should feel that they have earned fair commissions and clients should feel that they got what they paid for. Never make the mistake of taking a client for granted. Oftentimes, if not careful, agents tend to do this with friends or referrals.

Make the same quality presentation to all clients and follow through with what you say you will do. Quality work not only gains the respect of current clients but also gains future business through referrals.

The added value section of the book is written in a modified outline form for reference and application as needed.

Seller's Agent Added Value

How does a SELLING AGENT add value to the process?

For a SELLER

Defines the selling process, including:
Pre Presentation
-    Marketing Plan

o   Research the property

Before attempting to present to a potential client, an agent should know all facts regarding the property and as much about the seller(s) as possible. The first step is to research the history of the property by using MLS and tax records to understand what properties are selling for in the neighborhood and surrounding areas. It is also important to understand the trend of the property and the neighborhood. Is the property increasing, decreasing, or stable in pricing? Also, is the property competitive with other like properties and how does it compare to new construction in the area? Does the neighborhood add or subtract value from the property?

Exercise...

Use your current property or a familiar property as an example.

Address of the property _____

1.   List or print out from your MLS properties for sale in the same neighborhood
2.   List or print out from your MLS properties recently sold in the same neighborhood
3.   List the same information for two similar nearby neighborhoods
4.   List the same information for two new construction projects that will compete with the property
5.   Compare all the data to determine a target listing price for the property

Most agents do not include the similar neighborhoods or the new construction in their research nor do they try to determine if the neighborhood is increasing, decreasing, or static in price. When you know all the information, you can better determine the list price and have data to justify your target number to the client.

After completing this exercise, what new information did you learn about the property you researched?

How could you use what you have learned to your advantage?

The objective of this exercise is to cause an agent to become more knowledgeable about a property than competing agents.

o   Plan a preliminary marketing strategy
You cannot plan an effective marketing strategy without good data. In the last exercise we learned how to extract the data necessary to present a factual and effective presentation to a client.

What other media should you have in hand to present to a client?

Clients make their decisions to list with an agent based on the agent, the agent's company, and the presentation. Excellent agents know how to outperform in all three areas.

Before considering the presentation of material, picture yourself in front of a prospective client. Try to see yourself as if *you* are the client. What do you feel/think?

Be as honest with yourself as possible and ask, "How would I rate my appearance? Is it appropriate and professional? What message does my appearance send to the client(s)? Would anything about my dress offend a husband or wife?"

Does my appearance suggest trustworthiness? If not, what does it suggest?

Now ask, "What do I need to change in order to make the right impression on a client and how would making the change increase my chances of listing the property?" Once the personal assessment has been completed, the process can begin.

The Process...
-    Develop an event time line

Exercise...

What are the events that occur between offer and closing on behalf of a **seller**?

_____

_____

_____

Which of these events are common to most or all transactions?

_____

_____

_____

Establishing a Time Line for Critical Events

A time line is a calendar of events that must occur between initial offer and completion of any transaction. The time line should be written down with all significant events recorded on it. Focusing on a time causes both the agent and client to explore and define not only the issues that must be addressed but also the plan to address them.

The objective of establishing a time line and discussing it with a client is to:

- Show the client what will be involved in the process of selling the home.
- Help the client clearly understand how much you really do to earn his or her business.
- Raise the bar for other agents competing for the listing. Make them commit to what they intend to do for the client.
- Demonstrate that you are familiar with this process and that you are committed to this level of service.

Time Line Example

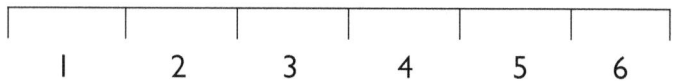

1	2	3	4	5	6

1. Offer
2. Negotiation
3. Time line for critical events, i.e. inspections, completion dates
4. Final inspections
5. Closing date

In order to ensure that each critical event occurs at the appropriate time, agents must train all parties to the contract regarding their roles or duties in the process.

The purpose of training all parties to the transaction is to prove that, as an agent, you are the expert and are capable of managing, thus gaining trust and respect. The benefit is a managed transaction from initial contact to closing.

Exercise...

Build a time line for a seller

What can you learn from Exercises 1 and 2?

_____

_____

_____

How can you apply what you have learned?

_____

_____

_____

What results will you achieve from applying what you have learned?

_____

_____

_____

Premise:

According to studies, 75% of real estate clients hope to hire someone to manage the process. They do not have the time or desire to become knowledgeable about real estate.

- Presentation

o Tour the property with the prospective client

The most important step of the presentation is to tour the property with the client. Ask the client to point out the positive and negative attributes of each room of the property. Be sure to ask why each attribute is important.

The purpose of asking about each attribute is to cause the client to:

- *clearly understand that you care*
- *begin to develop a more realistic picture of the property*
- *invest time and both emotional and logical energy in the process*

After investing time in your presentation, the client will expect other agents to invest also. They will probably eliminate agents who skip this part of the presentation.

The objective of the property tour is twofold.

- The agent and client establish a mutual understanding about the property.
- The agent builds trust and value because he or she demonstrates both concern and knowledge to the client.

Action is much stronger than words. Walking through the property while proactively asking and listening creates a much stronger impression than sitting at a table with unsubstantiated list pricing documentation based only on price per square foot from the MLS.

o   Ask questions

Ask questions that produce expected results. When you ask questions about problems with a property you will increase client anxiety. Always follow or precede a question that increases anxiety with one that emphasizes something positive about the property. At the end of the tour, you should have developed a list that will clearly demonstrate how the property will be seen by potential buyers. You will also have developed a list of repairs that will help present the property in the best manner.

The objective of this exercise, in addition to gaining valuable information, is to

- Gain control of the process
- Establish a working relationship
- Build trust

Questioning and Listening Skills

When asking questions there is a system to follow that will give you the information you need for future negotiating. **Always write down** the answers to questions as accurately as possible. Tape recorders or even typing on a computer still makes most people nervous and they stop answering. Decide what type of answer will meet your needs. If you ask questions that can be answered with a yes or no you will not get much information. If you ask open-ended questions, an expanded answer will give you much more information and some perspective of who the other person is. Open-ended questions begin with who, what, when, where, why, and how. Never ask questions that have no purpose. If you are working with highly logical people, they will ask you why you are asking the questions. Be sure that you clearly understand the answers. If you do not understand, ask for clarification or ask a clarifying question. When you ask questions, you will learn about the type of people you will be negotiating with as well as their needs and boundaries. Identifying needs and boundaries should be your objective, which you accomplish by asking pertinent questions and listening carefully. You should also have a clear understanding after clarification. Remember, when you accumulate enough information, stop asking. You might finish by asking if the other party or parties have any questions for you.

Example...

You go to a listing appointment. Should you begin presenting or asking questions? You might begin by asking, "What are your expectations of me if I list your home?" The client should understand the question and provide invaluable information. The agent will have an opportunity to discuss the process and be sure that the expectations are not only clear but also attainable.

If you begin to present prior to asking, you will be fortunate if you answer the questions the client has. It is a guessing game to try to negotiate a listing contract without knowing how to meet a prospective client's needs or understanding his or her expectations.

> Good questioning skills develops a plan for an agent to add value and gain client trust.

Asking good questions

- Ask open-ended questions to gather information.
- Ask close-ended questions to gain commitment.
- Never ask a question without a reason.
- Be sure you clearly understand the answer to the question. If you are not totally sure, clarify before moving on.
- If the question uncovers a potential problem, ask how the other party sees resolving it.
- Write down the answers.
- Ask if the other party has any questions.
- Mark the answers emotional or logical.

Listening skills must be developed by all people types. To listen effectively you cannot talk at the same time. You also cannot listen effectively when you are thinking about potential solutions while the other party is talking. You cannot listen to the needs of more than one person at a time. It is a myth to think that a person can process more than one thought pattern at a time.

Listening involves elevating the person talking to the highest priority. You must eliminate all other thoughts from your mind except what the other person is saying. Remember that if a client talks, what they say or ask is important and will not go away. Always address the issues immediately. However, be careful when answering to plan a strategy to get back on track once the issue is addressed adequately.

Example...

Have you ever found yourself listening to someone who stops and says, "Excuse me, but you have not heard a word I have said." In addition, you know that it is true. Developing the skill to listen intensely to what someone else is saying is difficult. There are some points that will improve the process of learning to listen.

Learning to listen

- Keep your focus exclusively on the other party
- Allow only one person to talk at a time
- Try not to allow yourself to think about solutions while the other party is talking
- Paraphrase what you think you have heard
- Ask if what you paraphrase is correct
- Ask questions if you do not think or feel you have understood
- Take notes if it is necessary for you to remember what is said
- Be sure the background behind the talker is not distracting
- Count to three after the talker has finished
- Maintain eye contact when listening unless taking notes
- Never interrupt

When it is your turn to respond

- Be calm
- Be aware of your tone of voice

- Be aware of your language
- Think and formulate your responses before you speak
- Be direct and complete with your response
- Clearly delineate one subject of response from another
- Ask if you have provided an acceptable answer
- See yourself as a partner in the solution and act like one
- Use words like "we"
- If you take an adversarial role, be sure that you have a reason for doing so

o   Present the marketing plan
The marketing plan should be a combination of

- the facts you have discovered about the property and location from MLS and tax records
- the information gathered from the home tour
- presentation of your qualifications
- presentation of the company's qualifications
- advertising, Web sites, and any other methods you will use to promote the property

At this point you will have presented all of the information necessary for the clients to make a decision to list with you. As you present each of the parts of the marketing plan, ask before moving to the next part if the clients agree with your conclusions. If they do not agree or are hesitant, spend time addressing concerns before moving on.

Example...

You have finished your company presentation and the client asks, "I have heard that your company does not represent properties in this area of town."

What do you say to overcome this objection?

_____

_____

_____

Possible answers:

I understand your concern and I'm glad you asked,

- Please understand that I would not be here if I did not think that both I and my company could and would represent your property well.
- We do not represent many properties like yours, which means that it will be given special attention.
- You have decided to allow me to present to you. Based on your concern, how did you come to that decision?

Listen closely to the answer because the clients will more than likely answer the question. Be sure that in asking your question you do not sound confrontational or uneasy about asking. Legitimate questions deserve legitimate answers that remove concerns.

Newer agents tend to dread the inevitable question that a seller will ask: "How long have you been selling real estate?"

Agents should always have an answer since this is a legitimate question that the seller should ask. It is important that the information an agent provides is accurate. Length of time in the business could be a real concern for the seller and needs to be addressed.

What are some possible answers you might provide that will cause the seller to be comfortable?

_____

_____

_____

If indeed the agent is relatively new, the only answer that will provide comfort is to develop a company story. An agent should have a reason for choosing the company that employs that agent. The agent should have a compelling story to tell to the seller.

Possible reasons:

- The reputation of the company
- The company's commitment to training
- The company's commitment to excellence
- Market penetration
- Market niche
- Commitment to listings
- Advertising
- Community visibility

An agent should select reasons that are not only important to him or her but also represent added value to the seller's listing with the agent or company.

Whatever reasons the agent selects, he or she should be so passionate about the reason for choosing to work for the company that any prospective seller would also choose the company.

As the agent matures in the business, it is still important to include the company story in each presentation. Clients see strength in a company that truly endorses teamwork as a benefit to their clients. If the agent begins to rely on self and cut out the company, he or she will weaken her presentation.

Questions to ask a seller to introduce the company

- Have you heard of Excellent Real Estate (sellers will probably respond with a yes so they can move on)?
- What have you heard about us?
- Would you feel good about listing with Excellent?
- What do you think Excellent can do for you that other companies cannot do?
- Why have you chosen to allow me the opportunity to list your home?

These types of questions reveal truths about how your company is competing in the market. If the answers are positive, it will become increasingly difficult for the seller not to list with Excellent. If the answers are negative, the negatives will have to be overcome or the seller will probably not list with you.

o Discuss the listing price and commission

Clients will usually try to rush to the listing price and commission as early in the process as possible. A client logically thinks that he or she should interview several agents in order to confirm that they are all alike. If the client does not determine that there is added value by one agent over the others, he or she will choose the lowest commission and highest list price. There are always companies in any business sector that even claim all companies and services are the same and that the commission paid is the only variable. If that were even remotely true, anyone would choose that method of selecting an agent and company. Be prepared to justify both the list price established for the property and the commission rate based on the facts you have prepared. If an agent is not able to demonstrate that he or she is correct on the list price and worth the commission, he or she will probably not compete effectively in the listing arena.

o Sign and explain documents

The majority of clients do not want to read or study the listing documents. Clients really want to focus on

- Listing price
- Commission
- Length of the contract

Clients want to bring the transaction to its simplest terms: the net proceeds and how long it is going to take to sell the property. If an agent has not built added value as well as understanding of the process, the client will compare agents only on the net and length of contact. Without a good presentation of the facts gathered to substantiate the list price and commission, the agent has not truly earned the right to represent the seller in the transaction. Securing the listing is a matter of the seller's perception that one agent will actually provide better service. Developing the perception is a matter of demonstrating, in some measurable form, exactly what is involved in representing the seller from list to closing.

Offer options; do not make critical decisions on behalf of clients.

- Post Presentation

The post presentation should begin after the documents are signed. An agent should at this point develop a time line based on the critical events of the process and explain the responsibilities of all parties in order to move on to closing. Agents should offer to assist in the process but should **never make critical decisions.**

Agents should always think in terms of presenting options as opposed to giving advice that influences a decision. The reason for presenting options is to clearly define any liability associated with a decision.

Example...

The seller says, "I want to list my home for $200,000. What do you think?" Your options are saying the property is listed too high, too low, or just right.

Think of some possible answers an agent might offer.

_____

_____

_____

The best answer is to explain the impact that the listing price will have.

Answer: "Mr. Client, I have shown you the facts regarding your home; however, it is your decision as to the list price. The supply of homes and demand for them in the market will actually determine the sale price. What will happen is one of the three options.

1. The listing generates an immediate acceptable offer on the home.
   This is the desired result and we move forward.
2. The listing generates showings but no offers.
   The listing is generating showings. The agent needs to find out why there have been no offers and address the issue.
3. The listing generates no showings or offers
   The listing is probably not priced correctly to draw attention.

Any of these issues can be defined and addressed in order to sell your property.

o   Pre Inspections

Many agents now discuss the merits of "pre inspections" prior to listing. The purpose of a pre inspection is to define any issues that might surface after an offer and jeopardize a sale. Pre inspections also provide a seller with the ability to determine the cost that might be associated with any needed repairs and have a better idea of what he or she will net from a sale. Pre inspections also offer peace of mind to a potential buyer in knowing what might need repair or that all necessary repairs have been addressed. Pre inspections can include anything that would seem to impact the salability of the property. These issues will come up. Better to address them now than when they might be a "deal breaker."

o   Repairs

Once any pre inspection issues or repairs are identified and the client agrees to the repairs, the repairs should be made prior to listing if at all possible. The best opportunity to sell occurs as soon as the property is listed. The objective of making repairs is to cause the property to present better than other properties with similar qualities in the same price bracket with an added measure of peace of mind. If there are no identifiable issues of concern but the life cycle of appliances or heat and air are toward the end, adding a home warranty also addresses buyer peace of mind.

o   Interview showing agents for accurate feedback

Clients want feedback on their properties. Once showings begin, clients often complain about agents' lack of response. Agents should remember that clients become very anxious about cleaning and preparing for a showing. They expect a call back to understand what occurred and what they might do to generate an offer. It is easy to call back with positive feedback but difficult to call back when the feedback is not so good.

REMEMBER...

Ask the showing agent for specific information

- What was your impression of the property?
- What could be done to generate an offer?
- Is there anything the seller needs to address?
- What about the list price?

When asking pricing information, remember that if buyers are not interested in the property, they are not likely to evaluate the property as closely regarding price. Price is factored in only if the property is to be considered.

Feedback is twofold. An agent not only needs to know what the client thinks but also what the showing agent thinks about the property. The agent has probably shown the competition for the property to his or her buyer client. How did your listing compare to the competition? What is the competition?

o   New construction.
o   Within the subdivision.
o   Outside the subdivision.
o   Ask where the listing is on the buyer's short list? Is it in first place or where?
o   Ask what could be done to move it into first place.

A great response from feedback is "My client would have bought the property if…" Can "if" be changed?

Write down the feedback in the words of the showing agent. Be aware of the use of adjectives in the feedback. Adjectives inject emotion and detract from the logical issues of the property, although they are legitimate. Try to understand what the facts are, what issues can be fixed, and what can be done to change how the property competes. Some issues cannot be fixed and will probably impact the actual sale price of the property. Identify consistencies and inconsistencies in the feedback to determine any real problems.

o   Feedback to client

Clients say they want feedback when they really would prefer an offer or positive encouragement. Agents know that to be true and often try to soften negative feedback.

Presenting negative feedback should not be made painful but should be factual and encourage positive action from the seller if possible.

Feedback is, "We did not like the colors in the home of the walls or carpet."

How do you present this information the seller?

_____

_____

_____

The objective is to keep this issue from becoming emotional. Do not allow the seller to feel that objection to the colors in the home is an assault on him or her. Paint and carpet can be changed. Hurt feelings are another issue. First, determine if changing the colors would result in an offer from the buyer agent. If changes would result in an offer, ask how the buyer would want to address it. Would the buyer rather ask the seller to make the changes or settle on a cash amount to address the issues after closing? If addressing the colors is not going to generate an offer, it is now important to present the issue in as positive a light as possible.

You might say, "Seller, there is a concern about the colors of the walls and carpet in the home. If we continue to receive feedback indicating that this is the issue keeping us from an offer, we will need to consider our alternatives." Seller is likely to ask, "What are the alternatives?" At this point, an agent can offer options.

"Seller, the options, if the colors are indeed what is keeping us from an offer, are:

- Change out the carpet and paint the walls. If you choose this option, many carpet suppliers will allow you ninety days to pay. If the property closes during that time, you can pay for the carpet out of closing proceeds. This choice should eliminate the problem.
- Offer an allowance to a prospective buyer to make the changes. A buyer then has the option of controlling the choice of carpet and you know how much you are willing to spend up front. This choice does cause a prospective buyer to think that the colors are a potential problem because the seller has pointed it out by making the offer.
- Understand that someone will also like the colors in the house. You can choose to be patient and wait for the right buyer.
- You can also reduce the price of the house to try to overcome the issue. This may only result in a lower offer on the property. The question is will reducing the price to overcome the colors be effective in a lower price bracket?
- Offer

o Negotiate the offer

Think in terms of options and break down issues to the simplest equation. Do not allow a buyer to micromanage each issue of the offer but encourage the buyer to see the big picture.

Example...

You receive an offer that includes an addendum asking for personal property. There are quite a few items including a swing set, window treatments and even some furniture. Your seller appears to be uncomfortable with the list of items and the other terms of the contract.

How can an agent counteract the potential problem?

_____

_____

_____

Do not confuse a laundry list of personal property to the point that it jeopardizes the potential sale of the property. Ask the seller,

- Is there anything on this list that you would not sell?
- How much would everything on the list be worth to you?

This approach reduces the decision to "things for cash" instead of giving away personal items.

Once the value of the things is established, tell the seller:

Consider this approach; make a counteroffer with these options to the buyer.

- Buyer can have the items on the addendum for a sale price of $...

- Or the buyer can purchase the home for $... without the items.

If the price of the items has been determined to be $2,000, then the sale price of the property should reflect the amount in this choice.

The other option is that once a price has been established for the items on the addendum and the seller recognizes the worth, the seller may decide to view the items as simply a discount of the selling price that works for him or her and thereby accept the offer.

The objective is to help your seller see the offer as net dollars for his home in a manner that allows him to make a logical decision without feeling that he / she has to give away personal items to sell the property.

o   After the offer but prior to closing time line

What are the critical events of the contract prior to closing?

_____

_____

_____

Use the time line format to assist your seller in clearly understanding what is to be done and within what time frame. The agent can again offer to assist in the process as long as the assistance does not involve decision making. For example, the agent can assist in setting up a termite inspection and delivering the documents to the closing. The agent should not choose the termite inspector or negotiate any repairs.

o   Inspections

What inspections might be required from a buyer, at whose expense, and within what time frame?

_____

_____

_____

These are contract issues. The buyer has the right to conduct any type of inspection that he or she deems necessary to properly evaluate the decision to purchase as long as all parties to the contract agree to the inspections and the consequences of the results contractually and in writing. The buyer customarily pays but this is also an issue of contract between the parties to the contract. Real estate contracts have a "time is of the essence" clause in them and specific dates negotiated by the parties to the contract. It is important to position the inspections and completion dates on the time line so that they are met. There are consequences to missing dates for completion without extending the time frame in writing.

After inspections are completed, the buyer's agent will contact the seller's agent with whatever is requested by the buyer to satisfy his or her concerns.

All parties to the contract should have a clear understanding of the scope of the inspections and rights of each party. Sellers should be aware that most inspections are contingencies to the contract and usually give the buyer the right to negotiate for repairs within certain limits or to terminate the contract. Once the seller receives the results of the inspections and requests of the buyer, he or she will need to decide how to handle any issues of concern.

Many agents think that the best way to settle repair issues is by cash settlement. If cash changes hands there is little room for misunderstanding. If a seller agrees to make repairs, he or she is bound only to make the least expensive repair that addresses the issue.

Example...

A seller's property has a leak in the roof. It will cost approximately $200 to repair but $500 to replace the roof. What should the seller do?

_____

_____

_____

The seller would be required only to spend the $200. However, might the buyer choose to spend an additional $300 to replace? A cash settlement leaves the ultimate decision in the hands of the appropriate party.

The buyer also has the right to a final walk through of the property. You should be sure that the seller understands the buyer's expectations and can meet them appropriately

The buyer might expect:

- Everything out of the property
- To allow the seller extra days or time to move
- All repairs to be made or explained
- The property reinspected by the home inspector to approve repairs
- Any issues of the contract completed satisfactorily

The seller's agent should go over the buyer's expectations with the buyer's agent prior to the final walk through. Seller's agent should also contact the buyer's agent after the walk through to confirm that all issues have been addressed appropriately.

o Follow-up

Your client should have a copy of the time line so that it will be easy to follow the progress from offer to closing. Using a time provides the client with a sense of control of the process. All changes or even conversations can be recorded on the time line sheet for reference by the agent or the client. Using the time line also demonstrates, as the transaction progresses, that the agent has eliminated surprises.

- Pre closing

o Arrange the closing

Traditionally the buyer chooses the closing agent because most of the closing costs and benefits go to the buyer at closing. However, the choice is also a matter of contract and can be determined based on the needs of both parties as negotiated and stated on the contract. Once established, the closing date should be added to the time line so that all events prior to the closing can be completed in advance. When the closing agent is established it will be the seller's responsibility to communicate the necessary information to him or her. The seller's agent should provide telephone numbers to the seller and the title company to ensure good communication. Agents do not need to know the specifics of personal financial information unless it impacts the property transfer in a negative manner. If an agent does discover that the seller is going to have a problem with closing, it is the seller and seller's agents' responsibility to convey the information to the buyer's agent and buyer in a timely manner.

o Follow up on HUD

The seller, listing agent, buyer, and buyer's agent should receive a copy of the HUD statement prior to the closing.

When a HUD statement is received the agent should review the statement and contact the seller to confirm that the numbers are correct. Always ask the seller to review to be sure that there are no unanswered questions at the closing. If the seller has questions, the seller should contact the closing agent as soon as possible so that all questions can be answered and/or changes made. Seller questions usually focus on prorated items such as taxes or issues concerning payoffs that impact his or her proceeds.

Once everyone agrees that the HUD statement is correct, there should be no other issues to discuss at the closing table.

- Closing

If the time line is honored and attention given to all details prior to closing, the closing should be simply a matter of signing the papers and wishing everyone well. The seller should be able to leave with his or her money and the buyer with peace of mind about the property he or she has purchased.

However, sometimes sellers should not be at the closing for a variety of reasons.

- The sellers have moved and do not want to invest the time or money to physically attend the closing. If that is the case, it is the seller's agent's responsibility to follow up with the closing agent so that papers are sent out in time to close. It is also important to confirm with the title agent transfer of funds and any other details.
- The sellers are not on good terms. Sometimes divorce motivates sale of a property. It is improper

to expose buyers to sellers who are having problems like a divorce that should not affect the transfer. If this is an issue. Arrange for the sellers sign the papers prior to closing and not necessarily at the same time. Try to keep closings as painless as possible for all parties.

- Add both parties to contact list.

Most SELLERS would choose to focus on sale price, commission, and advertising.

Why?

_____

_____

_____

> *Most SELLERS would choose to focus on sale price, commission, time line, and advertising.*

Sellers want to hear that they can get the **highest** possible price and the l**owest** commission in the **shortest** sales cycle. They would also like to accomplish this without investing any time, money, or effort in the property to accomplish their goal.

There will always be an agent who will say, "I can do that!" in order to obtain a listing.

Knowing that someone will make the above statement, how does an agent with integrity cause the seller to recognize the reality of the situation and a get true picture? This problem will be addressed in the negotiating section.

For a BUYER and BUYER'S AGENT

The seller's agent can add value to the buyer/buyer's agent by focusing on the transaction. The principle is that sellers want to sell and buyers want to buy. Negotiating from both sides should focus on the principle until agreement is reached or the parties conclude that no agreement will be reached.

- Offer

o   Define and focus on objectives

A seller's agent can share any information that is pertinent to the sale with a buyer's agent that is permissible by the seller. While planning the marketing strategy with the seller, an agent should discuss specifically what should and should not be passed on to a prospective buyer or buyer's agent. A buyer's agent needs to know what to say to his buyer about the seller's property. It is the seller's agent's responsibility to supply information that will favorably promote the property.

How can a seller's agent supply information to promote the property?

_____

_____

_____

-   Flyers
-   Brochures
-   Presentation book
-   Notes about the property
-   A handwritten endorsement note from the seller

■　An endorsement note from the seller is a highly effective tool. After a day of visiting properties most buyers have problems remembering which ones they liked and especially what the liked about them. Anything that the seller's agent can provide that will remind the buyer about the property will help.

All buyers satisfy their logical needs and then make an emotional decision regarding purchases.

o　Big Picture

A seller's agent should explain to the seller what his or her options will be when the buyer makes an offer ***before*** any offers are received.

Sellers can,
- accept an offer
- counter an offer with a response
- reject an offer

The seller's agent's responsibility in presenting an offer is to keep focused on the facts of the offer and not become emotional. An offer is an offer. If the offer is low, the seller's anxiety level is bound to rise; the seller may say something derogative about the offer and simply reject it. The seller's agent should always ask the seller to allow a full presentation of the facts before commenting. After a full presentation, the seller's agent should go over the positive and negative points of the offer to determine the next strategy.

In some cases, when the offer is presented, the seller may be satisfied and simply accept the offer. The seller will usually ask his or her agent for an opinion. The seller's agent should respond that it is up to the seller to decide on the response without commenting on the good or bad of the offer. Even if the offer appears to be good in the eyes of the agent, it is still the decision of the seller without any persuasion from the agent.

If there are concerns by the seller regarding the offer, the agent should go over each point and determine

1. Is the point a deal breaker or something that can be negotiated?
2. What are the priorities of the issues? Some will be more important that others.
3. Which points are negotiable?
4. Which are not?

Once the offer is clearly defined, the agent should understand how to present a counteroffer. It is important to go over how the counteroffer will be presented so that the seller understands exactly what will be conveyed to the buyer's agent to tell the buyer. The objective is to develop a script to convey what the buyer's agent will **repeat** to the buyer in words that will cause the buyer to accept the counteroffer. Feed the buyer's agent with exactly what to say to his or her client. Keep focused on the fact that the buyer is interested in buying or would not have made an offer.

Example...
On a property listed at $300,000 the buyer offers a purchase price of $200,000 and asks for ninety days to close and $1,000 closing costs.

The seller thinks this offer is entirely too low, does not want to lose ninety days of marketing time and thinks $1,000 is too low.

What are the seller's options?

_____

_____

_____

The seller could reject the offer. However, if the seller chooses this option does he even give the buyer a chance to change the terms? A flat rejection often terminates any negotiation toward a contract.

Always encourage the seller to counter the offer. If he or she chooses to counter what are the options?

_____

_____

_____

If the seller begins to counter the offer, often the transaction ends up at "half live" or about equal distance from the list and original offering price. To keep this from happening, the seller might consider one of the following options.

- ■ Counter the offer by reducing $1,000. The objective is to see if the buyer is serious about the offer or not. Seller's agent should instruct the buyer's agent to tell the buyer that the seller is interested in selling but not at the offering price. The buyer's agent should be encouraged to go back to the buyer and tell him or her to raise the counteroffer.

- ■ Counter with the bottom-line price and instruct the buyer's agent to tell the buyer that this is the bottom line the seller will take.
- ■ Do not counter the offer but instruct the buyer's agent to tell the buyer to submit another offer if interested. Tell the buyer that the offering price is just too low to begin the negotiating process.

The selling agent should know that the buyer's agent must present any offer on behalf of a buyer. The seller and seller's agent have no way of knowing what the buyer will do with a counter proposal. The selling agent may have told the buyer that his offer is low and to expect a counteroffer. Many buyers like to test a seller to be sure that they are getting the best price possible. Also there are many "self help" books that encourage this type of strategy. Consider the offer as valid and do not give up until it becomes evident that the parties are too far apart to come to contract.

o Keep your eye on the ball, negotiate from a positive position

The agent's task is to stay focused on the transaction and present in the best possible manner while representing the seller accurately. A good counteroffer that leaves something on the table for the buyer has a strong chance of acceptance.

o   Position any offer with the buyer/buyer's agent

Try to counter in an either/or manner so that the buyer's agent can offer a choice rather than an opportunity to renegotiate the whole offer.

Example...

The offer on a $250,000 listing is $225,000 and $5,000 closing costs. The seller's agent explains that the closing costs are not the issue. The issue is a net sale price of $220,000 ($225,000 - $5,000).

The seller can accept $225,000. The offer should be positioned as follows to the buyer's agent.

Seller will accept $225,000. If the buyer needs $5,000 in closing costs, the acceptable price will be $230,000. Buyer's choice.

-    Post Offer
o   Stay on Track

Once an offer is accepted, it is the seller's agent's responsibility to stay on track and keep up with all details that need to be coordinated with the buyer or buyer's agent. Once the negotiating process is completed and a contract agreed upon, all parties to the contract should be working **together** toward the transaction. If this attitude is maintained, everyone builds trust and the closing will be smooth. The seller's agent should view the buyer's agent and the buyer as partners and treat them with respect while expecting adherence to the terms of the contract.

o   Manage the details

Follow up on all the critical events between contract and closing with the buyer's agent. Give a copy of the post contract time line to everyone so that there are no surprises and to assure that everything is finished (inspections, releases of contingencies, repairs).

- Closing
o Follow up on details

Refer to the time line and make notes of contacts and decisions. Update the time line periodically to all parties. This demonstrates the agent's professionalism and covers the question of responsibility and accountability for finishing any duties.

- Add both parties to contact list

Seller's agents sometimes forget to add the buyer's name to their client list. If an agent has performed well, why not ask the buyer for referrals, etc. A seller's agent never knows about the satisfaction level of the buyer. They may want the same level of attention that has been demonstrated the next time they sell. If an agent has demonstrated that he or she is different, the agent may have earned business later if he or she remembers to ask.

Want vs. Need

During communication between clients and an agent, the agent, through good listening skills and questions, must begin to determine if the client is talking in terms of wants or needs. The difference in a want and a need is that one is much more emotional than the other. Wants are less tangible or measurable and often expressed using words of a feeling nature.

Illustration...

When the agent asks what the client **thinks** about a home, the client says, "It just does not feel right." If the agent is listening to the response, the agent should recognize that he or she has asked for a logical answer and received an emotional response. After a few questions and responses, the agent should begin to understand how emotional the decision will be. Depending on the nature of the agent, the question and answer might be reversed. The agent might ask, "How do you **feel** about this property?" The client might respond, "I think the home is not a good value." One question and one answer do not establish a pattern but multiple questions and answers will.

The purpose of understanding the nature of the questions and answers is to establish a comfort level for mutual communication between the client and agent. The comfort level can be defined as the area where anxiety is lowest for all parties. An agent can measure when he or she is approaching the boundaries of comfort by a change in the client. Changes include:

- Body language; the client begins to look or act more tense
- Language; the client's language becomes more defensive
- Language; client uses fewer words
- Tone of voice; changes
- Answers; become evasive or client changes subject

When this occurs, the agent can either ask questions that are less invasive to move back into the comfort area or continue on carefully and patiently if the information is necessary for understanding that the agent is approaching the end of the comfort area or moving completely outside of it.

Exercise...

What are your comfort words when communicating?

_____

_____

_____

Do the words vary depending on the subject?

_____

_____

_____

How do you explain the change in words depending on the subject?

_____

_____

_____

The reason that people change the words is that they place a higher priority on some decisions than others. The priority is usually based on how much risk the decision represents to an individual.

Illustration...

In a real estate decision the agent must help clients understand what factors will have an impact on their decision. Again, how much logical information the clients will need to feel comfortable will depend on their emotional and logical needs.

As an example, assume that the market favors the buyer and there are quite a few available properties meeting clients' needs. Also assume that there has been quite a bit of news coverage that presumes the market favors the buyer to the extent that the buyer should be able to negotiate an extremely favorable deal for any property on the market.

The problem here is that the perception of the market is not 100% accurate. In any market great properties priced correctly will sell and not have to be sold at distressed pricing. Also, in any market distressed properties are a problem at almost any price level.

The clients find a home that they really **want** but **need** to be sure that they do not overpay for the property.

Exercise...

How should the agent proceed and what should he say?

_____

_____

_____

Remember that agents should provide options and not make critical decisions. The agent should develop a market analysis for the property to try to determine a fair market value for the property. The analysis should then be weighed based on the factual and the emotional attributes of the property. Questions like:

- What is the condition of the property?
- What, if anything, makes it unique?

- How many other choices are available that closely match this property?
- How does it compare to other properties the client has evaluated?
- How much does the client want this particular property?
- How closely does it meet their emotional and logical "perfect home" picture?
- Can they afford the home at list price?
- What do they want to offer for the property?
- Are there any favorable terms the clients can offer, such as a flexible closing date?
- Are there items that the sellers want to convey with the property?

What other issues might factor into the decision?

_____

_____

_____

The spectrum of the decision making could be across the board from emotional to logical at this point. The reason for the question/answer consideration exercise is to allow clients to become comfortable with the decision by verbalizing to the agent and hearing him work through his thoughts.

The highly emotional, after considering the property, might say, "This is the perfect property (even though the market indicates that an aggressive offer is appropriate), and we want this home even if we have to pay full price."

The highly logical person might say, "This home meets my needs; however, if I cannot get it at the price I have in mind, I am prepared to consider other properties."

Buyers and sellers will eliminate their concerns if they are given the appropriate information to make the decision.

Agents can influence a decision depending on the information they supply to the client. It is important for the agent to balance information in order to allow the client to make a non biased decision.

Information given to a client can be balanced between the benefits and consequences to a decision.

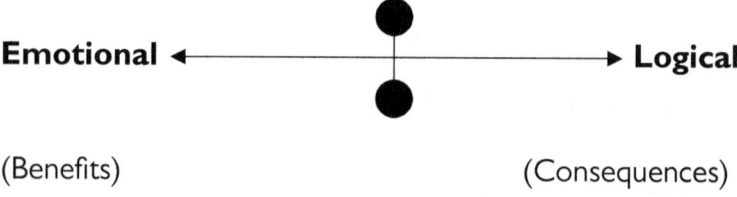

Emotional ←——————————→ **Logical**

(Benefits)   (Consequences)

An overbalance to benefits will appeal to **highly emotional** people. These types see benefits as support of decisions and will not want to hear about consequences to decisions they want to make.

Overbalance to the consequences as opposed to the benefits will appeal the highly **logical types**. These types want to know exactly what all the consequences are as presented in an unemotional manner so that they can make the right decisions. They are comfortable weighing in benefits, but only after they have thoroughly evaluated the consequences. These types are likely to stop the process if the consequences cause concern, even if they would like to proceed.

HINT... When presenting to these types, do not use many adjectives. These types think that adjectives are injected purposely to distract and are used to try to manipulate their decisions.

i.e., ... "This is a *great* offer." Or "This is a *bad* offer," when, in fact, an offer is simply an offer.

> *No one likes to be fire hosed with unnecessary information.*

Overbalanced to the logical types want a fair representation of both the benefits and consequences. These types want all the information available in order to understand how to negotiate to their advantage. They will factor both the emotional and the logical into an offer and expect the offer to be presented to the seller in a way that both emotional and logical factors support the offer. These types want to present an offer that is difficult for a seller to turn down from the emotional and logical positions. These types would present an offer saying something like, "Now you know that..."

Overbalanced to the emotional types tend to want a balanced picture of the wants and needs. These types will use the Ben Franklin approach and make a list to see if the wants outweigh the consequences. Support by the agent in answering questions honestly will help these types with decisions.

Once an agent understands how this works, there is a temptation to influence a decision by overbalancing to the emotion or logic of the client. What that means is mirroring the client instead of balancing the emotion and logic of the decision. After all, a client will be most comfortable with questions, answers, and information that support what he or she wants to do. Only the personal integrity or ethics of an agent will determine how information is used or misused.

Negotiating the Decision

A *professional real estate agent* will work hard to master understanding how a decision is made including:

- People's tendencies and how their makeup influences decisions
- How to determine availability of product
- What adds value not only to the product but also what the perception of value is
- Adding self-value by understanding and explaining just what a professional real estate agent does for a client

Once the agent has gained the personal knowledge necessary to perform successfully he or she can apply the facts and the perception to serve the client effectively and efficiently.

A good grasp of fact and perception is good; the wisdom comes in how to properly apply the information. Some people will need quite a bit of information, others may need very little. The agent who performs well knows what enough is and what too much information is. It is easy for an agent to become so excited about what he or she knows that the client becomes overwhelmed. No one likes to be fire hosed with information that they do not need to factor into a decision.

So how does an agent determine the right amount of information? Part of the solution is based on how emotional or logical the client appears to be.

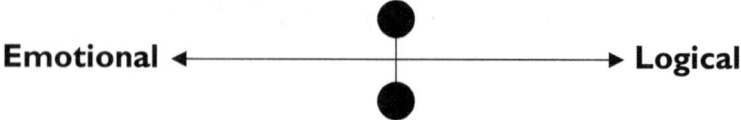

Emotional ◄————————————————► Logical

Determining what information is essential comes from the earlier section about asking good questions and providing good answers.

Negotiating the decision encompasses all the dimensions of the process of decision making and guiding the process to closure. There are many facets and much understanding that goes into mastering the process.

Defining the Decision-Making Box

The first step in guiding decision making is to define the comfort box of the client. The box consists of the facts and the perceptions that the client believes to be true and reliable in making a decision.

Illustration...

Agent Judy is working with the Joneses to help find a home. They are moving to East Tennessee from coastal North Carolina. The Joneses have never been to the area before but are excited about the move. Judy is conducting the interview and the Joneses begin to describe their dream home. They would like to move to a small farm and buy horses. They would like several acres of flat land with a stream, a barn, and a fairly new home of approximately three thousand square feet. The Joneses' budget is $500,000.

Exercise...

What additional information does Judy need to help the Joneses?

_____

_____

_____

Questions that Judy should ask:

- Have you ever lived on a small farm before?
- How familiar are you with the East Tennessee area?
- Are you living in a subdivision now?
- Are you both in agreement about the farm?
- Have you owned horses before?
- What, if anything, are you willing to compromise about your dream?
- Is the location of the farm in relation to employment, etc. important?

If the Joneses have lived in this environment before they will have a much better idea of what they want. If this is truly a dream, they may not have their ideal box very well defined. Sometimes when people are planning a dream, they do not have the appropriate facts to define their box very well. What if Judy knows that it will not be possible to meet the picture that the Joneses have painted from an availability or financial perspective? If the clients never visited the area before, their perception of what is available may be out of line. People from a flat area think in terms of "flat land," not the hilly topography of a mountain area.

It is the rule and not the exception that people will describe properties they are familiar with from the area they know. It is unlikely that they will know what to expect if they are moving to an unfamiliar area of the country. They want to work within the box of familiarity since the idea of a move to a strange place represents enough of a loss of control.

Agents often find themselves walking a fine line between what clients would like to have and the reality of what they can acquire in a different market within their financial means.

How can Judy help the Joneses, whom she is just meeting by telephone, move outside their decision box this early in the transaction?

_____

_____

_____

It is most important at this point to try to direct honestly and politely without shattering the clients' dream. Judy might say, "I understand what you would like to accomplish in this market. How have you decided on what you want and your budget?" Judy needs to gently help the Joneses understand that they might have to compromise somewhere if their budget is not going to be enough to make it happen. Judy might also discover that the budget can be increased if the Joneses find the dream property. This is a very common situation where the emotion of the dream will become confronted by the logical reality of the budget.

What will be the final outcome? It depends of whether emotion or logic will prevail. Judy's job is to try to determine what she needs to show the Joneses in order for them to make appropriate comparisons and decide what action they will take. Judy will need to show several types of properties before even the Joneses will be able to know what they are going to do.

The decision box will always be somewhat of a moving target, factoring what people want versus what they can have. The agent must listen carefully to what clients say as they begin to redefine the decision box. Redefining will result in questions to the agent that will allow demonstration of the agent's knowledge and ability to interpret how the clients' compromises are thought through and how to apply new solutions to the adjusted decision box.

Illustration...

A couple has asked Scott to help them find a property within their budget of $900,000. The wife wants a well-appointed newer home in an upscale subdivision. When Scott talks to the husband, he wants ten acres and a barn for the same amount.

Obviously there are two entirely different decision mind-sets to work with.

Exercise...

What should Scott do?

_____

_____

_____

The issues might change but this not an unlikely scenario. The two people have completely different perceptions of what they want.

Scott might choose to identify two sets of properties and show all of them to both parties. There is no way Scott will be able to know how the decision boxes will merge until he shows the properties and listens to the couple respond to each other's needs.

Scott must be very careful not to take sides as the decision box merger begins. A couple with very different needs will often try to pit the agent on one side or the other. They try to create a two-against-one scenario so that one of them can win.

If this occurs, Scott will need to declare immediately what his position is in the decision process.

Remember...

Agents should provide options but not make decisions on behalf of clients. Scott should say something like "I am not the one who will be living in this house, you two need to decide what is going to make both of you happy!" The couple will understand that Scott is not going to play this game and will be able to focus better on the decision they have to make and what the acceptable compromise will be.

Understanding the decision-making box is the foundation of negotiating a decision. If the agent does not understand and define the box, how will he or she help move outside of it?

Asking questions and defining the answers is how the box is defined. Different types of people will ask questions differently and their answer will be different. The chance of miscommunication between different types of people can be minimized if the tendencies of the client and agent are both considered.

When asking questions, the issue of boundaries and directness can be a problem for the **highly emotional**. The questions from this type of person will be more along the line of:

- Do you like the home?
- Do you want to see more?

Vague questions do not require direct answer or provide closure information. These types of questions provide opportunities for more conversation without commitment to closure.

When answering questions, this type does not like to feel that he or she is being interrogated. It is best to let the emotional talk and evaluate what he or she is saying and ask questions that inject direction or focus. Sometimes it helps to offer a summary of what the highly emotional has said and ask if you are correct. This allows the client to hear what he or she has said and confirm accuracy. It may seem that there is little continuity with answers from this type. An agent must be patient, listen carefully, and ask questions that focus on the process.

Illustration...

Agent Bill is showing homes to a buyer client. The client is very talkative and likes the first three properties visited. Bill asks, "Which of the homes do you like best?" The client says, "I like all of them. This trip is highly productive and I can't wait to see some more homes!" Bill says, "That is great. Help me understand what you liked about each of the homes."

The client says, "They are all great!"

Exercise...

What type person do you think Bill is?

_____

_____

_____

What can he do or ask?

_____

_____

_____

If Bill is also a highly emotional, he may like the idea of showing more homes until the client finds one of interest.

The **overbalanced to the logical** person will ask more direct questions with the purpose of moving to a decision. Questions like

- Specifically what do you like about this house?
- How does it compare to the others?
- Would you make an offer on this one?

Direct questions that require taking action work best for this type. This type does not like to waste time and perceives the showing process as what needs to happen to make a decision.

When answering questions, this type will give answers that assist in minimizing investment in the process and meeting his or her needs.

Illustration...

Joe has shown a client three homes and asks, "What do you like about each of the homes and how would you rate them if you were making a decision to buy one of them?"

The client says, "I like them but have not seen enough to make that type of decision."

What should Joe do or ask?

_____

_____

_____

What should he not do?

_____

_____

_____

Joe should listen to the client and back off what could be perceived as impatience or pressure by the client. Joe needs to do what the client asks and show more properties, However, Joe needs to ask again about specific wants and needs to focus the client on buying a home, not looking at them.

Highly logical types ask the most direct questions with little emotion in the questions or the tone of voice. Questions like:

- Does this home meet your needs?
- Why or why not?
- If not this property, what specifically are you looking for?

These types listen more than answer. When they answer, they like answers that are focused and do not use a lot of words. They like the same type of questions. Sometimes they will reverse questions; i.e., if an agent asks, "What do you think?" they might respond with "What do you think?"

Illustration...

Susan is at a listing presentation. She asks the client, "What are your thoughts about the listing price?" The client says, "You are the professional, what do you think?"

Exercise...

What should Susan do?

_____

_____

_____

What type do you think the client is?

_____

_____

_____

If the client is a highly logical, Susan should show the client the statistics of the written market survey; the information should be presented logically and based on the facts. If value is to be added or subtracted, Susan should be able to support why. After Susan finishes, she should ask if the client has any questions or concerns and then ask again, "What are your thoughts about the price?"

Overbalanced to the emotional types prefer to listen and evaluate rather than ask questions. Their good listening skills enable them to understand the information the client is providing to them. They ask questions based on what they hear to clarify clients' needs and wants,

questions such as:

- That is interesting, can you tell me more?
- Did you say that you liked the kitchen?

When these types answer questions, they like to think before verbalizing their thoughts, especially if they have not had time to establish trust. They want to be sure that their answers are accurate.

Illustration...

Jane is making a listing presentation and asks her prospective client, "Have you thought about a possible listing price?" The client says, "I am not sure, tell me what you think."

Jane explains to the client the market information and asks again, "What do you think about the price?" The client says, "I need to sell the house for (dollar amount), do you think I can get that?"

What would you do next?

_____

_____

_____

Depending on the price that the client has provided, Jane needs to spend a little more time establishing comfort with the client. Jane should remember that when she agrees to the price, unless she expresses concern and discusses what will happen if the price is too high, the client will think that Jane has promised that the house will sell for the list price.

The point of this information is to show that the different types of people ask and answer questions differently. When different types encounter each other, there can be a problem in communication and perception of each other and expectations of the process. People are most comfortable with others who think about and perceive situations in the same manner. Trust level is high because there is mutual understanding of the process and method as well as familiarity. The decision-making box is the same and much of the unknown is eliminated. It is easy to understand why this situation is comfortable for most people.

The problem is that if an agent can be successful only with someone just like him or her, the agent eliminates most of the potential market.

To be successful in working with people, it is critical to understand the different tendencies and tailor presentations to meet their emotional and logical needs.

Clients often envision the real estate process as similar to crossing an unknown landmine field. They prefer to travel with someone who has crossed successfully before and follow them through.

Exercise...

What do you think when a highly emotional encounters each of the other types including another highly emotional?

Repeat this exercise for each of the other people combinations.

_____

_____

_____

What can you learn from this comparison?

_____

_____

_____

How can you apply what you have learned?

_____

_____

_____

How will applying what you have learned cause you to be more successful?

_____

_____

_____

Managing the Unknown

Managing the unknown causes people to be pushed outside of their decision-making comfort box and generally, they do not like it. In real estate, it is critical that agents have the knowledge and confidence to lead clients into this unfamiliar area. Clients often envision the real estate process as similar to crossing a landmine field. They prefer to travel with someone who has crossed successfully before and follow them through.

If an agent can establish this kind of trust with a client, the process should result in mutually satisfactory results.

Think in terms of how people with different tendencies react to managing the unknown.

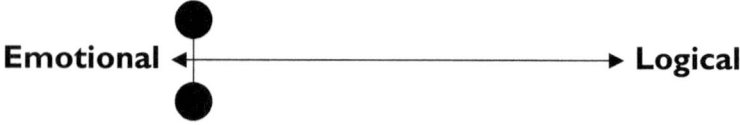

Emotional ◄──────────────────────► **Logical**

Highly emotional types do not fear the unknown; they find it to be a bit exciting and high energy. Since highly emotionals do not define boundaries well, their decision box does not recognize when the area of unknown is reached. Agents may find that if the client does not recognize the unknown very well, that it will be difficult to help clients understand how the decision needs to be made and the possible consequences or benefits. These types generally want to forge on through the process seemingly fearless of the unknown until it is time to make a decision and bring closure. The adventure through the process is more interesting than finishing. Finishing is like ending a book to these types and they can tend to drag out the process until it seems they have lost focus on closure. An agent has to try to keep these types focused on the fact that ultimately a decision will be necessary or they will not bring closure themselves. Options can be misconstrued as confusing. Agents should keep options clear and not provide so many that the decision becomes difficult.

Overbalanced to the logical types recognize the unknown well and do not fear it. They calculate the unknown and how it works to their benefit. These types are likely to define the consequences and benefits well. Agents will gain respect from these types by providing strategies as to how to manage the unknown by using both logic and perception. They are fine with the decision making in the area of the unknown; they expect agents to provide enough information for them to arm themselves to function effectively in this area. If agents cannot provide the information and appear uncomfortable in the unknown area, these types will lose confidence quickly. These types value confidence under fire and expect it from anyone they employ or use. Closure on their terms is the goal of these types. If a short time line favors them that works. If they see dragging the process is wearing out their opponent that works too. Winning is important and the agent who can provide a winning strategy is of optimal value to these types. These types want to work with those they deem to be winners. Closure is not a problem once these types get what they want. These types expect to be provided all options that they can use to benefit themselves.

Highly logical types isolate the unknown with facts. These types believe that they can eliminate the unknown area of a decision by identifying the facts. They respect an agent who can provide the facts to cover the area of the unknown. If agents cannot provide the necessary information, these types see them of no value. They would never venture outside of their decision box without solid evidence that to do so is wise. Verbal seldom gets their decision especially if they are expected to take action without proof. Once these types obtain the necessary information and they have established confidence that they know what the right decision is, they will move to closure. It is important for agents to stay focused and on track with these types. When they ask questions or want facts, agents must provide exactly what they ask for. Too much information or too little information is not acceptable to these types. They are highly focused and expect those who serve them to understand what they want and do it. These types do not waste much time on rapport or relationship building with those outside their trusted circle. Once their logical needs are satisfied, these types will make a decision. They expect agents to keep them in the loop but take care of the details for them. They like to clearly understand options for making decisions.

Overbalanced emotional types try to understand the area of the unknown and both the benefits and possible consequences to venturing into this area. These types will expand their decision box into this area if they have the facts to justify the decision. They may ask the same questions or validate the same information more than once to be sure that they make the right decision. These types will often use the value scale method to make decisions in the unknown area. They like to clearly know both the benefits and consequences and determine which is greater. This process takes time and may have to be evaluated several times to make sure that clear understanding has been established. If the consequences outweigh the benefits even slightly, it is unlikely that these types will proceed. Closure is not so much the problem as is being sure of the decision. Overbalanced emotional types expect agents to be patient and able to supply the right information as well as define the perception issues in a way that makes sense. They carefully evaluate both the facts and the agents as sources of the information. If they feel that an agent is misleading them in any way, they will probably not complete the transaction with that agent. Trust is of the highest importance to these types and is demonstrated with patience and honesty from an agent. These types expect agents to provide the options and opinions of what the options mean in terms of benefits and consequences. They may require that agents talk through the options with them. They will place value on what agents say and follow what they think is good advice. Agents must be careful not to over advise and allow clients to arrive at their own conclusions within their time frames. Agents who appear to be available but not too aggressive are welcomed by these types.

Hidden Agendas

Unfortunately, agents sometimes fall unexpectedly into clients' hidden agendas. Hidden agendas can range from misunderstandings between the parties to the transaction to outright fraud. As soon as agents realize clients have been dishonest with them, they should disconnect from the process to protect their reputations as well as avoid legal consequences. In many states, involvement in fraudulent practices can result in loss of license, legal consequences, and the possibility that E & O insurance may not cover the issue.

It is more likely that an agent can begin work with a client and immediately recognize the true picture of what the client is trying to accomplish or avoid.

Illustration...

Mr. Bryant has accepted a position that requires a move to Jane's market. Agent Jane is meeting the Bryants to show them property. The Bryants have provided information about their move and their needs and Jane has properties to show them. As the showings progress, Ms. Bryant does not like anything she sees even though the properties appear to meet the Bryants' needs. Ms. Bryant begins to talk about how much she loves her current home and the fact that she is so close to her family who all live within blocks of each other.

She also says that the properties she is visiting just do not meet the standards of her current home.

Hidden Agendas poison the communication process as well as undermine understanding or problem resolution

---

Exercise...

What is Ms. Bryant telling the agent?

_____

_____

_____

What can the agent do?

_____

_____

_____

What would you predict will happen in this case?

_____

_____

_____

In this illustration, what actually happened is that after complaining about all of the properties the Bryants visited, they finally settled on a property. The property was a new home that allowed Ms. Bryant to choose her carpet and paint colors. Once the selections were completed, the Bryants left to finish the move details, Upon return to close on their new home, Ms. Bryant said at the walk through, "The paint is all wrong and must be completely redone." The painter confirmed that the paint was exactly the color and brand that Ms. Bryant had picked. In order to appease Ms. Bryant, Mr. Bryant agreed to repaint the entire home at his expense. Six months later, Mr. Bryant called Jane back to re-list the home. He tells her that the former Ms. Bryant has moved back home. He is selling the property and looking for a smaller condo to meet his current needs.

> Buyers want to buy and sellers want to sell. All negotiating strategy should focus on the goal of completing the transaction until either the buyer or seller decides to terminate the negotiating.

Even the best of agents cannot fix every problem, especially the ones emotional by nature. Sometimes, even though difficult, agents must focus on meeting the logical needs as disclosed by their clients the best they can.

Managing the Negotiating Strategy

Agents must not only understand the tendencies of clients but also their own comfort area in order to determine the roles and duties of the negotiating strategy.

Again good questions and good listening skills will be the best way to forge the negotiating strategy with clients. The different types of people will want to assume variable levels of participation and control over the negotiating process. People will not be satisfied with the process if the agent is not able to determine or willing to submit to the needs of the client.

Remember...

Buyers want to buy and sellers want to sell. All negotiating strategy should focus on the goal of completing the transaction.

Negotiating occurs at the edge of the decision comfort zone. Good negotiators know that success occurs when all parties move into the zone where decisions can occur.

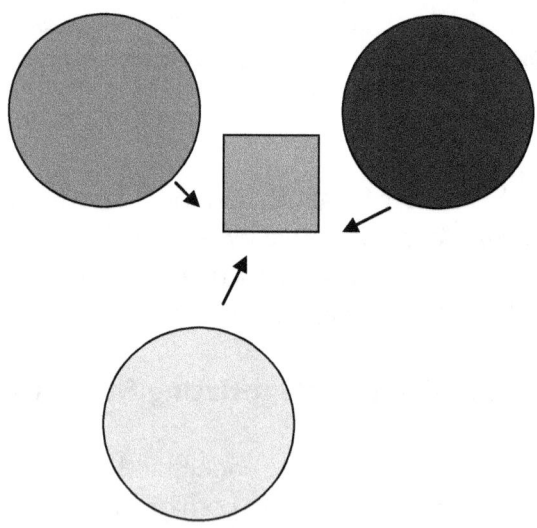

- What are the issues that a buyer will have to consider regarding negotiating an offer?

_____
_____

_____

- What are the issues that a seller will consider?

_____
_____

_____

Generally, in a real estate transaction, the big pictures are the same for buyers and sellers.

- Price
- Terms
- Closing time

Each of these issues can provide an advantage to either party.

With various personalities each will have different needs regarding planning the negotiating strategy.

When an offer is generated most buyers will ask what they should offer and most sellers will ask what they should take.

Agents should discuss the offer process after the listing is completed so as to prepare sellers for the options that will be available when an offer arrives. By having this conversation early, sellers can focus on how to negotiate the options. Agents should have a similar conversation with buyers as an offer is prepared so that buyers will understand their options if the offer is countered. The amount of strategy discussed with buyers or sellers will depend on what tendencies clients have.

Illustration...

James has just completed the listing agreement with the Smiths. They ask what is next.

James says, "The best that could happen is that we enter the listing in the MLS service and immediately a full price offer with acceptable terms is submitted. We take the offer and move on to closing. The next best thing that could happen is that we receive an offer that does not quite meet your price or terms and we negotiate with a counteroffer and finish with a contract acceptable to all parties. The third scenario would be that we receive an offer that for some reason cannot be turned into a contract and we end up rejecting the offer. You might give some consideration in advance as to what you might compromise if we need to work out an offer that initially does not meet your needs. I do not need to know the compromise but you should give it some thought."

If the Smiths were the buyers instead of sellers, as the offer is completed they might still ask the same question, "What is next?"

James should explain the options in a similar manner. "The best that could happen is for the seller to accept the offer as submitted. Their other option would be to reject the offer, which is highly unlikely. The third option would be to counter your offer with different terms or price. If that happens, you will need to give some thought as to what your response might be. You need to think about the maximum you would feel comfortable with paying for this property so that if you cannot achieve what you want, you will be able to move on to other properties."

How would you explain the options to a seller or buyer?

_____

_____

_____

Remember...

Agents also have personal tendencies and they will address these illustrations differently based on their particular comfort areas. There are no absolutes on how individual agents present to clients.

If the agent explains the next options, the seller or buyer will be able to focus on what **will** happen next. The agent has eliminated the anxiety of waiting for something unexpected to occur and replaced it with a plan of action. When a counteroffer occurs, the client is ready to move forward instead of having to take time to think about what to do. He or she already knows what action to take. The process will move more smoothly because the strategy for negotiating is already in place.

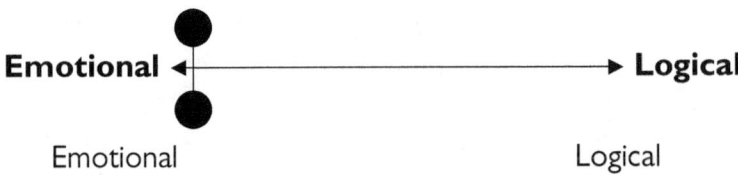

Highly emotional types will prefer the agent to handle the details of the negotiating on their behalf. These types will say something like "I trust you to handle the process." It is important for an agent to remember that these types are used to deferring decisions but often suffer the consequences of not staying involved. These types suffer from unfulfilled expectations that were never communicated very well. Agents should recognize that once the decision is made to proceed, a minimum amount of explanation is necessary.

For both buyers and sellers, an agent needs to always, as stated before, provide options and not make decisions or influence the decision-making process. These types will appreciate the fact that this approach removes some of the anxiety without their having to make too many decisions before presenting the offer. They will understand the process and they will prepare in advance for the next step.

Overbalanced to the logical types will also agree to this plan. They may want to make the most aggressive offer and it is important for them to be prepared for the next step. These types will try to appear to be firm on their terms and they may be willing to move on rather than negotiate much in order to establish a favorable position. As buyers, these types will have a more elaborate plan to get their way. They appreciate any direction that they perceive to provide an advantage to them. In reality, these types are willing to negotiate longer and negotiate back and forth if it helps them achieve their goals. They might adopt a strategy of making an offer and, if a counteroffer is extended, they might choose to wait a few days to allow the seller to fester about it before offering a response.

As sellers, this type will also be comfortable with negotiating several times before a contract is obtained. They might not give up all they could on the first counteroffer.

If an agent encounters a buyer and seller of this nature in the same transaction, the agent or agents must be sure that they understand and do exactly what their respective client tells them to do. These types like to control the process and exercise options as they choose. They will not appreciate it if their agents do not follow the plan they have agreed to, especially if they think something has been done without permission and it costs them the deal.

Highly logical types will appreciate this plan in that it will be perceived as limiting the options and defining them in advance. If the highly logical types do not agree with this plan or have questions or concerns, they will prefer to work out the details at this time in the process. This process also provides the highly logical with a perception of control that is comforting. This process also makes logical sense and provides solid ground for negotiation. If there is a negative side for the highly logical, it would be that if the negotiating process seems not to exactly fit into the process, they may feel that they were not provided accurate information and lose some trust in the process.

Overbalanced to the emotional types feel secure with this process. They may have questions that help them define what will happen; however, they appreciate elimination of part of the unknown. These types, like the others, will always appreciate a plan. These types also will appreciate the opportunity to invest time in how they will make a decision in advance. The advantage to an agent is that these types would be the most likely to need time to evaluate when an offer is received. By explaining the options in advance, their type will not feel under pressure when decision time comes. They will be much more likely to immediately respond to the offer.

Establishing Leadership of the Process

- "Lead, follow or get out of the way." Is a quote credited to Thomas Paine and could not be truer than in leading a real estate transaction.
- If everyone will focus on the transaction, success usually follows is also a good goal for agents.
- If you have to tell people that you are a leader, chances are that you are not.
- People follow those who are willing to not only lead, but are smart enough to share in the successes and shoulder the defeats.
- People follow leaders who demonstrate that the followers' best interest is foremost, not their own.
- Leading is a responsibility, not an entitlement.
- Leadership depends more on trust than knowledge.
- Followers surround themselves with trustworthy leaders.
- Leaders constantly get quoted regarding things they did not say or do.
- Leaders always are perceived as successful if their followers get what they want.
- When followers or other leaders reveal truth about themselves, leaders acknowledge the revelation by rewarding with trust.
- Trust is devastated by denial or misrepresentation of the facts by the leaders or the followers.

"Lead, follow, or get out of the way." Thomas Paine

The question is who will lead and why will the other parties defer to the leader?

The answer is the person or persons who have the best grasp of the process and are willing to take the lead. Shared responsibility is the best possible situation where the buyers and sellers address the issues in a manner that best serves all parties. This process is not meant to imply that either agent is to subordinate the best interest of his or her client on issues requiring negotiation or clarification as in negotiating the home inspection agreement to terms acceptable to both parties. Each type of person will have a different attitude about what role in leadership is preferable. Each type is capable of leading or participating at some level if he or she chooses to do so.

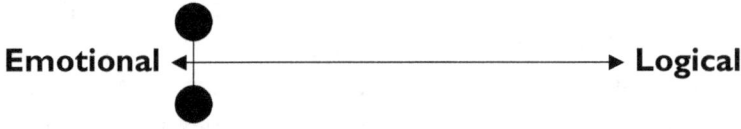

Emotional ◄─────────────────────────► Logical

Highly emotional types are usually interested in the leadership but may have trouble keeping on track with the details of the transaction. These types always like the idea of participating but may need guidance from someone to get the transaction finished. The inevitable issues that come into play during the process from contract to close tend to bore them and they can procrastinate until the last minute, especially if conflict on issues appears to a problem.

Overbalanced to the logical types will take charge of the process if allowed. These types often believe "if you want it done right, do it yourself." These types can be perceived as steamrollers and pushy by other participants in the leadership process. They can become irritable if they think others are not producing at their level or are not on the same track. These types hate the idea of looking bad because of someone else's perceived lack of performance. They are detail orientated and closure driven during the time between contract and closing. Overbalanced logicals choose the team of people who participate in the process like those from mortgage companies, title companies, and home inspectors that get it done and done on time. They like control of the process and prefer to be the leader whenever possible.

Highly logical types will also take charge. The difference is these types can become more rigid in enforcement of rules or contracts. Details rule in making any changes or decisions in the process between contract and closing. These types do not like changes during the process and want to work to the letter of the law. If it is agreed to in writing by all parties, then it is written in stone. Highly logicals are excellent in managing the details of the contract and process. Their inflexibility may make it hard for them to share leadership or focus on the transaction instead of a client's position.

Overbalanced to the emotional types will not choose to lead but are perfectly capable. These types tend to abdicate leadership but watch closely to be sure that all agreements are honored. These types will do what they commit to do and are good team members in moving from contract to closing. They will not sacrifice a client's position but are not as rigid as the highly logical, as aggressive as the overbalanced logical, or as disorganized as the highly emotional. This makes them easy to work with as long as integrity prevails from all parties.

Different types of people will lead from their respective strengths. Their success will depend on how they are perceived by their followers or other leaders. No matter what their strengths, people will follow only those who earn trust.

Trust is earned not by what a person says but by the action he or she takes. Only the leader who demonstrates confidence that he or she can deliver the desired results will be able to keep followers' attention for any length of time. In real estate, the agent who not only possesses the knowledge, but demonstrates the ability to apply it, will usually lead the process. Applying knowledge in a manner that is understandable and comfortable to a prospective client and that respects the client's decision-making process will establish the trust necessary for the client or other leaders to comfortably concede or agree to share the leadership role.

Leadership in the real estate transaction involves the ability to provide optional logical solutions when problems, concerns, or conflict become apparent. Leaders address the issues immediately and do not procrastinate. Leaders can focus on resolution without sacrificing their clients' best interest. They understand that if it becomes apparent that a client should not complete the transaction, there will be other opportunities to sell or buy.

Illustration...

A buyer has purchased a home and on receiving the home inspection, becomes concerned that there is a vague reference to a problem with the roof.

How should the buyer and his agent proceed?

_____

_____

_____

1. Hire a professional to assess the scope of the problem.
2. Determine the cost to fix the problem.
3. Decide on a solution.
4. Communicate the solution to the seller.
5. Negotiate a common solution.
6. If no common solution is possible, terminate the transaction and find another property.

The buyer must be in control of the outcome of this process. The agent should provide only guidance through the process. At each step, the buyer should clearly understand the options and decide whether to continue to try to secure a suitable solution or terminate and begin the process of finding another property.

The seller's agent should also be thinking about options and possible solutions. If the buyer determines that the roof issue is repairable and offers to accept a cash settlement, the seller needs to seriously consider the offer. In reality, if the seller chooses to settle the issue, he can meet his goal of selling. If he chooses not to make the repair and terminate the contract, he will probably still have to address the repair and begin the sale process again.

One can see how tricky leadership becomes when the different types represent different parties to the contract. In most real estate transactions, there is the possibility of six different perspectives represented not including the other service vendors to the transaction. What that means is that probably all types of people are represented in every transaction. From reading and thinking about these types in different situations, it is easy to understand how great the opportunity for misunderstanding or miscommunication is.

Most people think that they prefer to work with people just like…?

The answer is just like themselves. However, in most cases, people choose spouses who are completely different in perspective. Highly logicals choose highly emotionals as mates. As professional real estate agents it is important to understand how each piece of the process is interpreted by each type of person and recognize that the interpretation is likely to be *different*. With couples who may have totally different perspectives, needs, and processes for decision making, each person must be acknowledged and valued appropriately.

Exercise…

How would a highly emotional type perceive the highly logical type? What words would he or she use to describe the person?

_____

_____

_____

What words would the highly logical type use to describe the highly emotional type?

_____

_____

_____

Think about your personal tendencies. Which type would you work best with?

_____

_____

_____

Which type would you work worst with?

_____

_____

_____

If there are multiple types of people buying and selling real estate, what do you need to understand in order to work better with the ones who cause you trouble?

_____

_____

_____

When working with other agents, what skills, knowledge or perceptions do you need to change in order to work better with other types of agents?

_____

_____

_____

What is your leadership style?

_____

_____

_____

Are you satisfied with your role in leadership?

_____

_____

_____

If not, what can you work on to become better?

_____

_____

_____

Periodical self-evaluation is always a good thing. It causes people to look objectively at what they are doing successfully and what is causing problems. Even the most professional agent can get caught up in bad habits that need to be changed. Before any change can be made, habits need to be identified and a reason for change needs to be established. People do not change unless there is enough personal motivation based on some plan that establishes the change as overwhelmingly more valuable than the old habit.

Problem Resolution

Problem resolution and negotiating involve much the same process. The difference in the two is the position of the negotiator/problem solver. Negotiating is viewed by many as gaining an advantage, whereas problem solving focuses on eliminating obstacles to completing the transaction. Agents can assist in the negotiating process as well as problem resolution by providing options and following a client's instructions.

Problem solvers in real estate stay focused on the big picture and view problem solving as part of the process with the purpose of eliminating obstacles to bring closure to the transaction.

Some people confuse problem solving with conflict and can become uncomfortable with the process. Problem solvers define problems as opportunities to add value or as just part of the process to be addressed as soon as the problem is identified.

Once clients and agents understand that problem solving is a process with defined steps to conclusion, they become more comfortable and are able to effectively resolve problems.

The problem-solving process:

1. Ask the other parties to the problem to define it exactly.
2. What are the consequences the problem is causing?
3. What needs to be done to resolve the problem?
4. Agree on the solution.
5. Take appropriate action.
6. Determine that the problem has been resolved to all parties' satisfaction.
7. *Close the gate.*

Illustration...

The home inspection report identifies that the roof has leaked at some point. The leak does not appear to be a major issue to the buyer. However, the buyer asks the agent how to proceed.

Exercise...

If you were the agent, what would you recommend?

_____

_____

_____

Remember that an *agent should offer options, not make critical decisions*. In this case, making the decision could result in liability on the agent's part.

Possible options:

1. Tell the buyer that the leak is old and is not a problem. (**Wrong!!!**)
2. Recommend that the buyer consult with a qualified roof repair person and determine the scope of the problem.
3. Require the seller to fix the roof.
4. Require the seller to contract a qualified roof repair person to assess and repair the roof.

Possible seller options:

1. Agree to fix the roof.
2. Agree to contract to fix the roof.
3. Have the roof assessed and offer a cash concession to the buyer in lieu of fixing the roof.
4. Offer a cash concession without obtaining a professional opinion.
5. Refuse to address the roof problem.

Is there a best approach to this problem?

Other than the agent determining that the roof is not a problem, all the rest are possible solutions based on the original contract and the position of the buyer and seller.

Probably the best solution for all concerned would be to agree to a cash concession. By this agreement, the seller meets his responsibility without future liability regarding the repair.

The buyer can do as he chooses with the cash.

The problem with seller repairs is that the seller is only obligated to provide a minimal fix to the problem. There is a strong possibility that the expectations of the seller and buyer regarding the repair will not be the same. If the buyer accepts cash, it will become the buyer's responsibility to hire a contractor that will address the problem exactly as the buyer thinks it should be addressed. Also if there are warranties associated with the repairs, the buyer would be working directly with the warranty provider.

Think about how this illustration is addressed by the problem-solving process. Think about a recent problem you needed to resolve. How would applying the problem-solving solution have helped?

Would your results for solving the problem have changed for the better?

How and Why?

_____

_____

_____

Closing the gate is important because it establishes closure in

- Problem resolution
- Questioning
- Any process
- Any step of any process

Closing the gate means that before proceeding, always ask a question that gains a closure answer.

- Is there anything else we need to discuss?
- Are you comfortable to proceed?
- Did that fully answer the question?
- Is the problem solved satisfactorily?
- Do you feel good about the solution?
- Is anything unfinished?
- Are there any unanswered questions to address?
- Can we proceed?

These are very direct questions that establish focus on how to proceed to closure. The questions accomplish:

1. No more time or energy need to be invested in what is before the gate.
2. There is a reason to proceed.
3. Intent to close is established.

The next question is, "What else needs to be accomplished?"

This question establishes a checklist to clearly define what is still on the table to be resolved before closure. Each contact with a client should be defined by asking or understanding

1. What was accomplished at our last meeting?
2. What do we intend to do today?
3. What are the expected results?
4. What will be left?

Between meetings it is appropriate to assign homework to one or all parties. If homework or outside activities are established before a meeting, it is easy to measure the commitment to the process by the quality of the homework. The homework will be something like, *at the next meeting, I will be prepared to...*

No matter what type of people types are involved, managing the transaction depends on gate closure to keep focused and produce desired results for all parties.

Myths about Real Estate

1. Real estate agents make lots of money easily.

> If buyers or sellers do not know what is true and what is myth, it is the agent's duty to explain the difference.

Real estate agents can make a lot of money but most do not. Why do most **real estate agents** fail in making enough money?

- Poor time management skills
- Poor client skills
- Selfish; self before clients
- Do not apply themselves
- No business plan
- No goals
- Poor money management
- Think it is easy money

All of these issues play a part in why most agents do not make "lots" of money. If money is the primary reason people choose real estate as a career, they will make their decisions based on money. Clients quickly figure out that they are just a "trip to the bank" and resent it. Integrity suffers when money is the first or only priority. If money is king, how to make it is all that matters. There will always be a way to make money. The more important objective is developing a plan to keep it. There is always someone interested in helping a real estate agent part with money. Advertising, training, car expenses, and taxes are all a drain on an agent's cash flow. The perception that real estate produces easy money is the most self-defeating attitude of all. By the time new agents figure out that they will starve if they do not produce and that playing golf usually does not produce income, they are usually too far in the hole to continue in the field.

The way real estate agents make "lots" of money is no secret. They

- Work hard
- Plan smart
- Invest wisely
- Manage their time
- Value their clients
- Study the market, are considered experts and professionals by clients and peers
- Stay engaged in real estate activities
- Give back to the community

When agents focus on providing excellent service to clients, the money usually takes care of itself.

2. Agents work only when it is convenient
This is possibly a true statement. However, the statement is true only when applied to clients. Most successful agents find that once they establish a reputation for quality performance and professionalism, it is more difficult to limit the time investment than not. It is important for a successful agent to have an interest that takes time away from work and do it.

Illustration...

A person from a prominent real estate firm called me and asked if I would assist in training the firm's sales team. When I asked what they hoped to accomplish, the response was that they wanted all of the agents to increase their volume and, as a result, make more money. When I asked how much they made on an average, the manager said each made in excess of $1 million. I said, "That seems to be very good. Why are you not satisfied with that number?"

They had decided that if they hired someone to train the team that some magic would occur and the team would increase the volume and thus their income. I asked what action the company would take if the team did not increase volume. Would they fire these agents? The manager said, "Oh, no, they are the best in town. If we fire them, they would immediately go to work for our competitor."

I told her to save her money. The team had reached a level of income that provided well for their needs and they were now doing what people who have achieved that level do; enjoying some of the fruits of their labor. Most people work so that they can do something they like in addition to work. If they do not have an outlet or spend some time with family members, they burn out or end up divorced and lose the money anyway.

3. Clients are liars; the do not tell agents the truth

I personally hate this expression. Sometimes clients do bend the truth but I have found that most of the time, when I hear this response and ask a few questions, I find that there has been either miscommunication from the client or a mismatch of people types. How as agents can we expect clients from different markets to communicate in terms they understand and it translate perfectly to a market they have never visited? If an agent listens and asks patiently, most clients will provide the best information they are capable of communicating. It is the responsibility of the agent to translate the information given by a client into what works in the agent's market.

4. Real Estate Agents save the best deals for themselves

This seems to be a concept that has migrated through the media to buyers and sellers. Nothing could be further from the truth. The way this has been presented is that agents encourage sellers to take the first offer even if it does not fulfill all of the needs of a seller. It has also been implied that agents hold out longer for a better offer. **Question...** how could this statement possibly be documented? Most agents will say that a seller should always consider any offer and try to work out the details whether it is the first or the last. In fact, the offer that is accepted and closes is always last, regardless of whether it is the first or twenty-third offer. Good agents see offers as just that; they always try to explore all options until negotiations fail to cause the deal to work out. Agents assume that once an offer is extended, there is a buyer who wants to buy and a seller who wants to sell; the objective is to work out the details so that both end up with what they want.

5. They make too much money for what they do

This misconception stems from the perception about how the earned commission is distributed. Most clients have no idea what kind of investment working in real estate requires. Advertising, education, license fees, transportation, signs, and supplies are all real expenses. A real estate agent is actually a small business sharing certain costs with a broker and a group of agents to defer certain fixed costs. Anything earned would be too much without knowing what the cost of business is for an agent.

6. The listing agent gets all the commission

Many sellers still think that they are providing an opportunity for the listing agent to sell their home. I wonder sometimes if sellers think that buyers' agents show people around just because they enjoy looking at nice houses with no expectation of compensation. Savvy agents include some type of information as to how the earned commission is distributed in order to educate their clients. If agents know that this misconception exists, it becomes their duty to educate clients in this area.

7. All Real Estate Agents do is drive nice people with model children around all day

The most interesting aspect of this myth is that it is probably the least important part of a professional real estate agent's duties. For a buyer client it is most important and they may not even realize that out of the thousands of properties available in a given market, the agent has already invested quite a bit of time to try to ensure that the properties visited will come as close as possible to matching the established wants and needs of the buyer. The average buyer visits fewer than twenty homes before making a decision. That number would represent much less than one percent of available properties in a given market. The objective of an agent is to show the right number of properties for a client to obtain the logical and emotional comfort needed to make a decision. No more and no less information is necessary.

8. *Real Estate Agents get to look at nice houses*

Have you ever listed or sold a foreclosure or a rental property? If you have not, please visit a few before attaching any credibility to this statement. Most buyers prefer to see only the best of the best. Remarks like "needs tender loving care" or "sold as is" eliminate most qualified buyers unless they have very specific needs. Agents show what their clients want to see, which usually does represent the nicer homes. However, agents who have been in the business for any length of them have seen it all; the good, the bad, and the ugly.

9. *An individual can sell the property better without a real estate agent*

The only seller who believes this to be true has:

1. Never tried this before
2. Been very lucky
3. Will never do it again after experiencing what a real estate agent does.

Agents cannot usually talk people out of trying to sell their property "by owner." Most are polite and remind prospective clients that if they cannot sell real estate themselves in a given amount of time, that the agent would at that point be glad to list the property.

The pitfalls of this decision:

1. People knock on the door unexpectedly.
2. People are allowed into the home without screening.
3. Many of the people who visit for-sale-by-owner homes are hoping that a miracle will happen and they will somehow be able to buy the house, even though qualified people have told them differently.

4. If an offer does occur, who will complete the paperwork and move the offer to closing?
5. How does the seller qualify the buyer?
6. How does the seller keep the buyer from experiencing buyer's remorse, feeling that the seller was not totally truthful about disclosure of negative aspects of the home?

The positives of this decision:
1. The seller could **possibly** save some money

10. The listing agent will sell the property

This myth must be addressed during the listing presentation. Many sellers still do not understand the process and think that the primary role of the listing agent is to **sell** their property when the actual statistic is that this happens only 20% of the time. If this is the expectation, the seller will lose confidence in the agent almost immediately and probably change agents unless a quick sale occurs. The seller must commit to the listing agent's ability to **manage** the real estate process as described in the prior material. If an agent is successful in communicating the process of managing the transaction, the seller can separate how to evaluate the performance of the agent even if the property does not sell immediately.

Most agents do not like weekly calls to sellers when activity is low or feedback is negative, especially if these calls continue for any length of time. If the commitment to communication is based on evaluating the marketing process, there will always be something positive to address. The seller should understand that the **process** can be evaluated and changed at any time without changing agents.

11.The listing agent will always show the property

The seller not only expects the listing agent to show the property, but becomes dissatisfied if other MLS agents show it instead. If the seller believes this myth, they do not understand the management process and that the listing agent's role is to manage the showings and feedback. The listing agent's goal is *for* other agents to show the property. Sometimes sellers will request that the agent be present for all showings. Before making this commitment, the listing agent must explain why this is a very limiting method of marketing the property.

However, before the agent begins to address this issue, the agent should ask questions about **why** the seller makes the request. Most of the time this seller request for an agent to be present stems from a bad prior real estate experience.

1. Something stolen from a prior property
2. Doors left open
3. Gates left open
4. Alarm systems set off or left off when the property is shown
5. Concern about valuables or medications in the house
6. Concern about pets
7. Concern about children
8. Concern about how the property will be presented (special or unique features)

Whatever the concerns, the agent needs to listen carefully and offer solutions to the concerns if they are actually relevant. Sometimes the fact that the agent is interested enough to listen and offer solutions will allow the seller to minimize the concerns and agree that agent presence at showings is not necessary. At least the agent should point out to the seller the downside of the commitment:

1. Scheduling showings may become a problem
2. Some qualified buyers might not be able to work within the schedule

After any and all concerns are addressed, the agent must decide if he or she is willing to make a commitment to be present at showings.

12. Real estate agents drive the best cars and pay no taxes

That would be great, but not true! Most real estate agents drive vehicles that are comfortable for their clients. Many agents who show raw land drive four-wheel drive SUVs, not because they like using lots of gas, but to serve their clients. As for the tax issue, agents are entitled to the same tax breaks of any small-business owner. I have never had an agent list tax relief as a benefit of selling real estate. This myth stems from the same thought that agents make lots of money and do not work very hard to earn it.

13. If a property does not sell immediately, the solution is to fire the listing agent

If an agent does not explain what he or she does and how that adds value to the process, then this is a logical solution. An agent must provide the seller with a plan to sell the property that allows the seller to evaluate what is happening during the process and not just wonder what the agent is doing. If an agent does not explain the plan and how value is added, then the agent will usually not have an opportunity later to explain.

14. Seller believes that if the house does not sell it is the agent's fault

Also stems from poor presentation planning and communication during the listing presentation. The seller is willing to listen and negotiate during the listing presentation. After the fact, the seller can interpret the agent's attempt to explain the process as an excuse for poor performance. Whatever the seller thinks the agent has committed to do becomes an expectation and is used to evaluate the process. Sometimes sellers even think and base expectations on prior experiences. Prior to beginning the listing presentation, agents should ask prospective sellers, "Tell me about your prior selling experience. What did you like?" Next question should be, "What did you not like?" With answers to these questions, the agent can understand and commit to or negotiate the expectations of the seller to mutually acceptable performance standards.

15. Real estate agents just make up the list price

Who came up with this idea? The seller who says to the agent, "What about a list price of $$$?" And the agent responds, "Sounds good to me. Let's sign the paperwork and get on with it." If this myth has validity with any seller, then it means that prior experience with selling homes has not included a professional presentation of facts. Most agents understand how to produce a competitive market analysis from MLS numbers. The presentation would fail only if the agent did not understand how to present the facts and then add or subtract value based on the other factors affecting the list price. The truth is that real estate agents justify the list price based on reality. Sellers may not be able to handle the truth for a number of reasons.

1. Their financial situation may not allow them to sell for the market value.
2. Neighbor Bob has told them what their house is worth.
3. Uncle Ned from Ohio who went broke as a builder ten years ago has provided a market value target price.
4. Another agent has provided an unrealistic target price.
5. They used an Internet site to determine the list price.
6. The seller has bought a new home without a contingency to sell. The buyer contract has a closing date thirty days from acceptance by all parties. However, the currently owned property has to net a certain amount to meet the terms of the purchase contract.
7. The spouse living in the house during a divorce does not have to move until the house closes and likes living in the property to be listed.

The professional agent must understand the non realty issues as well as the facts in order to assist in determining the market value list price.

16. The company pays the agent and the commission is a bonus

Not in my market. I discussed this with my broker to be sure that I was not the only one without this kind of contract. However, with the different marketing approaches to real estate today this plan may be available in some markets.

17. Real Estate Agents start late and quit early

This myth is stated incorrectly. Most real estate agents start early and quit late. Agents are more likely to work in the "chicken" syndrome, working from sunup to sundown. In the summer, when daylight time is extended, it is not unusual for agents to be showing property until 10:00 p.m.

18. The seller determines the list price; market conditions have no impact

Understandably, sellers would like to set the price to meet their needs. "Buy low, sell high" would be great for a client. However, the reality of this myth is also untrue. Market conditions dictate the base price of any property. Agents constantly face the challenge of justifying list price with sellers. No one wants to hear that they will make less on a sale than they expect. There is a strong tendency for sellers to list with whoever tells them what they want to hear. It is also difficult for agents to walk away from listings when sellers have unrealistic expectations.

The best approach is to explain to the seller that all agents and buyers have access to the same market information as the agent is presenting. The problem with a listing being too high is:

1. The property will not show well against competition
2. If the property is shown, buyers will see that it is not fairly priced
3. Buyers buy the best of the best in their price bracket
4. Valuable market time is lost

5. Even if an offer is accepted, the property might not appraise
6. Once the property begins to age on the market, agents lose interest or think something is wrong
7. Sellers become frustrated and blame the agent
8. Sellers believe that the solution to the problem is to change the agent not the price
9. The agent will invest time and money in a property that potentially will not sell
10. The seller will lose confidence in the agent
11. The seller will somehow believe that the agent, not the seller, set the price wrong

If an agent lists a property that he or she thinks is too high, the agent should explain the potential problems that will occur and establish a time line for reductions in price.

19. All real estate agents are the same

This has never been true but falls in the category of comparing apples to apples. Sellers would like to think that all agents are the same and therefore they can list based on what they understand. How much can I expect to get, how much is the commission, and how long will it take to sell?

How clients choose a real estate agent often defies logic. Most people think long and hard about hiring professionals to provide services. However, when it comes to real estate, which represents in many cases the largest portion of the client's wealth, they spend very little time. Statistics show that most people pick the first person who crosses their path when making the decision.

So how do people choose a real estate agent?

1. Referral
2. Someone they like
3. A friend
4. A friend of a friend
5. Someone's spouse
6. Someone's child
7. An agent they know
8. An agent who advertises
9. A solicitation
10. Internet research
11. A name they recognize

With the introduction of different approaches to real estate by different firms it is even more important for a client to clearly understand exactly what the different firms and different agents offer. Clients can now choose from a whole spectrum of services at different prices. However, if the claims seem too good to be true, they probably are.

Clients should check out presentations by prospective agents or companies as well as check with references to validate that a company or agent has a reputation for delivering what is promise.

Several presentations along with some reference checking should allow a client to understand the offers of services available as well confirm that the client expectations match up with the expected services that are to be provided.

Word to the wise: check it out before committing. A little time investigating up front can save an investment of time and energy without results.

20. Real estate agents will not tell the truth

Real estate agents actually have a high motivation to tell the truth at all times. Both the profession's code of ethics and real estate law strongly endorse truthfulness and honest dealings by agents with clients. Penalties for violations can result in fines and/or loss of license. Most real estate agents work very hard to develop a client referral base to ensure the future success of their business. Dishonesty or honesty tends to attach quickly to an agent's reputation. Most clients expect honesty from their agents as well.

21. Agents do not listen to what the client says

This may be a concern for either buyers or sellers, depending on past experience. Clients report that their number one complaint with real estate agents is failure to return telephone calls. An agent is never too busy to return buyer or seller calls on a timely basis. In today's world of e-mail or cell phones, even the busiest agents can find time to return calls.

Good communication skills and a healthy attitude toward problem solving will allow agents to feel comfortable with returning calls even if there are problematic issues to deal with. If the problem is not lack of communication skills or reluctance to confront problems, an agent needs to identify what it is and either fix the problem or change the habit that underlies the reluctance to call.

Additional Selling Myths

22. People can be talked into anything

This concept has never been true. The idea is really that because people do make decisions at the emotional level that a salesperson can skip logical needs and depend on the "want" to overcome logic without any need to address the logical issues. The assumption is that when clients show up, they have already made a decision to buy and that the salesperson only has to stimulate the desire to buy a bit to make the sale.

Even if a buyer does react in this manner, the buyer is highly likely to feel buyer's remorse and back out of the deal.

23. Buyers want truth and sellers can't handle it

This may be a true statement some of the time. However, like most broad statements, there are exceptions based on the personality of the buyer or seller and agent. Any time an agent depends on broad statements without asking questions to determine what the other parties to the transaction think and feel, there is a chance of misinterpreting the situation and making bad assumptions. Everyone wants to know the truth in order to make good decisions. How the truth is communicated, depending on the people and scope of the truth, is the issue. When presenting, the more adjectives that are used, the more emotional the presentation. Logic and fact presentations do not need adjectives. Agents tend to use more adjectives to soften truth. This may be necessary but agents must realize that with more words and adjectives, they may appear to be nervous and uncomfortable with the truth they are trying to present.

Illustration...

While writing an offer, the buyer says, "How do we write into the contract that the red wooden play facility that looks like a fort in the back yard behind the house under the tree goes with the house?"

The agent might suggest writing, "The play facility conveys at closing."

Keep it simple and use as few words as possible.

24. Good salesmanship always produces the desired result

The truth of this statement depends on how "good salesmanship" is defined. Different personality types would define good salesmanship based on their strengths. Buyers and sellers would base good salesmanship on meeting their expectations. A good salesperson seeks to understand the personality as well as the emotional and logical needs of the client first. If that is accomplished, and the client and agent communicate in a mutually beneficial manner, then you might say that salesmanship works.

25. If you can obtain a mortgage; it means you should buy it

Just because a mortgage can be secured, it may not be good logic to make the purchase. Many people have been convinced that if a mortgage is available, the financial institution is endorsing the purchase as a wise decision. "Funny money" offers are by design available to appear to remove the obstacle of wise financial planning from the decision-making process. "If you want it and can mortgage it, then why not buy it?" represents faulty logic. Any opportunity to purchase in the form of a mortgage should be clearly understood and compared with at least one other like product before proceeding.

Summarizing the myths...

The purpose of including these myths is to better understand how important it is to attain a working knowledge of both the fact and perception that agents regularly encounter. People do not understand the process of buying and selling real estate. They do not have a good plan in place to interview and select an agent or firm.

The agent must be able to understand the client, apply the knowledge, and formulate a plan that works for him or her to serve a client effectively. Most people have participated in some sort of customer service or people skill training at their place of employment. They recognize organization and professionalism and hope to benefit when they make any kind of purchase.

Illustration...

If you do not believe that people recognize and expect the people they deal with to provide them with service, ask several people to describe the last time they were served with excellence. They will probably have to think about it for a minute, but they will be able to describe the experience

Now ask if they remember the last instance of poor service. They will probably remember more quickly and describe the incident in even more detail.

People are not bashful about recommending good service or expressing displeasure about bad service to others.

Serving vs. Selling

In real estate, as well as in most other areas of service, old hard pressure or "glad-hand" selling is a thing of the past. People expect those who provide service to them to understand and have a desire to meet their needs. They also expect service providers to understand their products and how to help people understand their buying or selling options.

Real estate agents are also expected to understand how to lead and manage the process from the initial meeting or listing to the closing when one party gets a key and the other a check. Clients expect agents to assemble a team of professionals who can quickly and professionally eliminate any problems that appear between the time they visit properties until they own one. Agents should have a goal of appearing so professional that their client base looks to them even after the sale to provide the names of plumbers, electricians, cleaners, surveyors, and other providers. If a client thinks that the agent is actively screening providers on a regular basis for others, he or she wants to stay in contact.

The benefit for the agent is that these people are loyal and recommend others who are buying or selling real estate.

Every real estate agent has to make a foundational choice about whom he or she is serving that will define the agent's method of operation. There are three primary choices, although a healthy balance and respect for all three would be the perfect choice. Overbalance to one of the three is what tends to cause problems.

Agents can make money the top priority

This is the least effective decision that an agent or company can make. If money is the primary goal, all decisions and actions will be made on how much and how quickly one can obtain it. Often rules are ignored and values sacrificed in pursuit of money. This causes the agent to see clients as "a trip to the bank" and somewhere during the process the client will recognize the agent's motive by the actions and communication process. Serving money as a top priority will also have a negative impact on family and friends. If money is the priority, friends, family, and other commitments will be at the mercy of making money and there will be a constant reprioritization and loss of trust. Real estate provides an opportunity to work 24/7/365 if a person chooses to do so. If an agent is willing to make this kind of sacrifice, money will reward that person well but at a price to be paid back from the other components of life.

Illustration...

At a recent closing, the listing agent for the property, after receiving his commission check for more than $90,000 handed the seller a bill for $160 for lawn mowing. The seller took the bill, turned completely pale and told the agent, "We will discuss this later in private." The client's body stiffened and the table conversation ended.

Exercise...

Was the agent's action justified?

_____

_____

_____

Was the agent's action appropriate?

_____
_____
_____

What do you think the title company officer, the other agents, and the buyer thought?

_____
_____
_____

Why does it matter?

_____
_____
_____

What would you have done and why?

_____
_____
_____

Always think about the action you will take in advance and the impact it will have on others.

Agents can make self the top priority

If agents are in the business to serve self, their relationships with others will suffer as well. Like money-driven agents, self-centered agents will have little or no personal peace and often do not honor priorities involving others. Self-serving usually results in the "never enough" syndrome and people of this nature never have much satisfaction although they can seem to live very well. Always a better house, a newer vehicle, more travel, more "stuff" is available and seems to offer fulfillment until something newer or better comes along. This attitude about life in general as well as in real estate can be addictive. The "stuff" seldom provides any long-term fulfillment because there is always better stuff. Our society preaches through advertising that people are entitled to a constant flow of stuff and that they should feel bad about themselves if they are satisfied with what they have. People are also influenced by the idea that those with a lot of stuff are to be admired and have it all.

Illustration...

An agent has promised his spouse that they will go to dinner on Friday night. At 4:00 p.m., his client calls and asks if the agent can show a property at 6:00 p.m. The agent has shown the client several properties and, from the description of the property, the agent knows it is the right price and that it will probably sell quickly. The agent thinks, "If I show this property, I know the client will buy it and we can always go to dinner another night."

Exercise...

How do you think the spouse will respond?

_____

_____

_____

Do you think the agent's decision represents a pattern?

_____

_____

_____

What are the options for the agent?

_____

_____

_____

What option would you choose?

_____

_____

_____

What about the options that the agent could choose from.

1. Call his spouse and cancel dinner.
2. Call his spouse and schedule dinner later in the evening.
3. Offer to show the property now.
4. Offer to show the property later or the next day.
5. Arrange for another agent to show the property and split the commission in some mutually beneficial manner.

Any of these choices might work. Much depends on how the agent regularly makes this type of choice. If the agent has made his spouse a top priority and constantly reduces her to a second or third level, the spouse will quickly lose trust and respect. Constantly rearranging priorities starts with understanding, then moves to disappointment, and ends with distrust.

It is not so much what the top priority is as how an agent rearranges priorities without damaging personal and business relationships.

Agents can make serving others the top priority

Agents who serve others usually achieve good results and make a good living from their clients who know that they are important to the agent. These agent types make money, can reward themselves, and can usually achieve more balance in their personal lives. The issues of priority and how to adjust based on a bigger picture are clearer if this is the focus. However, these types, if overbalanced to others, can sometimes forget to take care of themselves.

Illustration...

An agent who always seems to have plenty of clients, volunteers for every job in every organization and seems to be the "go to person." However, while talking to some of his friends and clients, it becomes apparent that the agent has so many commitments that the agent seldom seems to follow through or show up for commitments. Everyone likes the agent but finds it hard to depend on him and slowly loses confidence. At some point, even his most loyal supporters will avoid business opportunities with this person.

For this type person it is important to learn to say no when over commitment occurs. The idea that no one else can do the job is not accurate and in reality these types sometimes keep others from opportunities that they could accomplish better.

Exercise...
What action does this agent need to take?

_____

_____

_____

Will the agent's attitude be easy to change?

_____

_____

_____

Balanced agents can balance all three priorities
Although difficult, agents can respect all three of these priorities and balance them all. Most agents have a desire or a need to achieve a certain income level. They also should work to enjoy the lifestyle that the income affords. All three of these positions can achieve success in their own way. When setting goals or planning, all three of these positional attitudes should be considered by agents to achieve some balance and greater satisfaction in their personal and business lives. A periodic review of goals and personal vision will help agents enjoy not only working in the field of real estate but also help them understand how to apply the benefits.

Exercise...

How would you evaluate your personal attitude in this context?

_____

_____

_____

Are you satisfied with your results?

_____

_____

_____

Are you satisfied with your life?

_____

_____

_____

If you decide to change something, what will it be?

_____

_____

_____

What results of changing will you expect?

_____

_____

_____

Are the results enough to make the change and form a new attitude?

_____

_____

_____

Everyone should complete this exercise periodically to ensure that practicing real estate is worth the effort and to prevent burnout from occurring.

Summary

Like real estate clients, agents have personal tendencies that have a strong impact on who they are and how they act. No one is going to perfectly apply all of the information, processes, or skills in this book. Think of the information as a tool box containing ideas of how to function effectively while achieving personal benefit from investing time and effort in the real estate field. It is more important to become more familiar with what works for you than to try to set a goal of "doing it right." People, market conditions, building techniques, and a host of other factors are constantly changing and affect the real estate climate. Agents must stay engaged with the market and with people in order to appear to be on top of their field. Real estate represents much more than listing and selling properties. Agents work every day to help people fulfill their perceived and logical dreams.

Pick and choose the tools that are appropriate for the situation and people you are working with as well as the tools that are comfortable for you. An agent does not need a jackhammer to drive a nail.

Learn how to identify what works for you and what is expected by the client. It is not about *what* you know but how you *apply* what you know.

"If you sit in a field on a three-leg stool and expect a cow to stop by and give you milk, it is not likely to happen." Real estate is similar in that you can learn about it, you can get ready to get ready, and you can identify potential clients. However, if you do not apply what you know, you will likely not end up with any milk.

About John Ritchie

FOUNDER; Real Estate Learning.com; BROKER / REALTOR®

QUALIFICATIONS:

- Founder of The Real Estate Learning Center located at www.realestatelearning.com
- Author of "The 3 P's of Negotiating...Exploring The Dimensions" approved by the Tennessee Real Estate Commission for 8 hours Correspondence Continuing Education, in addition, offered for continuing education credit via the Internet in Tennessee and for credit in 18 states through the National Association of Realtors®
- Author of "Needs Development, Negotiating and Presentation for Success", a general business application book released by Prentice Hall July, 2001.
- Contributing Author to "Negotiating for Real Estate Professionals", a program originating from The Women's Council of REALTORS® an affiliate of THE NATIONAL ASSOCIATION OF REALTORS® and DePaul University Center For Dispute Resolution, Chicago, Illinois 2003
- Author of "Adding Value Through Agency Relationships" approved for 8 hours continuing education by the Tennessee Real Estate Commission, 2006

- Certified Trainer by the Tennessee Real Estate Educational foundation in cooperation with the Tennessee Association of Realtors® April 2000.
- Author: "Building Productive Client Relationships" a sales/customer service training program including facilitation manual for train the trainer.
- Proven ability to develop successful marketing tools, business plans, training programs and administration policies and procedures for managing a successful growth organization.
- Qualified to mentor change at the Executive team or individual level.

EDUCATION:

- WAKE FOREST UNIVERSITY, Winston-Salem North Carolina, (1965 - 1969)
- Bachelor of Arts in Economics
- Additional concentration: Psychology / Sociology

INSTRUCTOR POSITIONS:

- University of Tennessee at Knoxville
- United States Office of Personnel Management
- Executive and Management Development Programs, Guest Instructor
- Roane State Community College
- Knoxville Association of Realtors®

BOARD OF DIRECTORS:

- Past Board of Directors; Knoxville / Knox County Leaders' Prayer Breakfast.
- Past Board of Directors; Fielden Business Furniture Group, Inc.
- Past Board of Directors; Smoky Mountain American Society for Training & Development, Knoxville Chapter.

PERSONAL:

- Past Area Class Administrator, Bible Study Fellowship International Tennessee and Alabama.
- Trainer, Knox Area Rescue Mission Drug and Alcohol Rehabilitation Program.
- Church Retreats and Church strategic planning.